Vera Bone
July 1972.

FLOWERS FROM FEATHERS

Flowers from Feathers

by Pamela Woods

illustrated by Michael Woods

DAVID & CHARLES

Newton Abbot

Acknowledgements

I would like to acknowledge the generous help of Tony and Leslie Birks-Hay, Gregory Parfitt, Judy Branston, and the Victoria and Albert Museum, London.

0 7153 5929 0

Set in 11/12pt Baskerville
and printed in Great Britain
by Biddles of Guildford
for David & Charles (Holdings) Limited
South Devon House   Newton Abbot   Devon

Contents

1 Feathers for Decoration   7

2 Types of Feathers   14

3 The Raw Materials: Preparing
the Feathers   23

4 Making the Flowers   30

5 Making the Leaves   88

6 Arranging the Flowers   111

7 The Fringe of Feathers   120

List of materials other than feathers   127

Index   128

Victorian hat piece

Ring-necked pheasant

I Feathers for Decoration

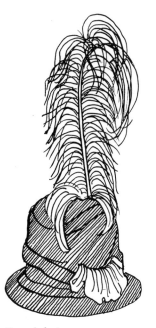

French hat, 1913

The feather excesses of the nineteenth century were in many cases locked away in trunks, and the happy gift of a chest of Victorian feather ornaments was partly responsible for my experiments in this form of flower decoration.

For some time I have been experimenting with dried grasses, seed heads and preserved flowers for house decorations in the winter months, adding artificial flowers made of paper and other materials to give excitement and colour to dried arrangements. I had sought to extend paper floral display to its limits with fantasy flowers and materials ranging from Japanese lacy paper to crêpe, cellulose and acetate film. Never, however, had I been able to find a patterned material which was any sort of substitute for the intricate detailing of even the plainest flower until I became aware of the beauty of feathers, and the strange affinity they have with plant forms.

Those people concerned with floral display will probably have experimented with artificial materials, especially for Christmas decorations, and will have noted with pleasure how paper flowers fail to wilt when faced with central heating at its fiercest, yet how quickly they succumb to dust. Too often there are those tragedies when, after a lot of work, a paper flower arrangement has been knocked over, and the result is a waste-paper basket full of damaged flowers. Feathers, however, turn out to be resilient things, however delicate they appear, and can be washed, dyed, shampooed and quickly restored to their first freshness.

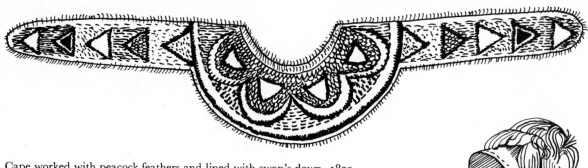

Cape worked with peacock feathers and lined with swan's down, 1830

Unlike paper, a large flat feather has enough detail in its composition to fill the area it covers with interest; the same area of paper would generally be unacceptably plain. The detail in the structure of a feather makes it a fascinating object under the closest inspection, and it has its natural organic resilience and curve—more often than not an asset in making petals and leaves which are so rarely flat in nature. Translucency is another quality which feathers share with petals, and the happy relationship with other natural materials can be seen on p 26, where the drawing illustrates a display made entirely from dried grasses, seed heads and feathers.

Flowers from feathers are easy to make, and few materials and tools are necessary. After a little practice, simple blooms can be made in about ten minutes, and a complete display in under two hours.

Until I came by my chest of Victorian feathers, I must confess that I knew very little about birds and their plumage. I soon took a careful look at the patterned feathers of pheasants and other game birds, and was astonished at the range. The individual patterns of different types of feathers are concealed on the surface of the bird by overlapping. Only their tips appear on the surface, and it is not until a feather has been shed that its beauty can be seen to the full.

For the average town-dweller, the collection of feathers for flower-making may at first seem to be a daunting and difficult task, but sources are numerous and the problem of collecting feathers is soon replaced by the problem of storing them. Wherever birds are reared for food there will be a supply of feathers to be had for the asking. Poulterers and butchers, especially around Christmas time, are often up to their knees in feathers, and only too pleased to give them away by the sackful. At other times they will usually keep the feathers of wild duck, pigeon and guineafowl if they know that there is an eager customer, and a sack of feathers will make a lot of flowers.

The garden is often quite a useful source of feathers, the more colour-ful wild birds like jays leaving behind beautiful plumage if you have the luck to find them. Zoos and wild life parks are a storehouse of exotic feathers, and here it is helpful if you can explain your interest and intentions to the zoo park keeper, who may be able to save moulted

Bonnet with ostrich feathers, 1830

Straw hat, 1908

Doll's hat with bird of paradise feathers, 1905

French skull cap, 1920

Fan made with feathers of the great argus pheasant

Fan with feather appliqué

Fan made of painted goose
feathers, 1864

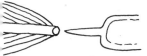

Details of manufacture of
fan

feathers which would otherwise be thrown away. Without his co-opera-
tion, the experience of seeing flamingoes preening themselves and Lady
Amherst Pheasants moulting inside their cages may be a most frus-
trating one for the feather-flower maker.

Most useful, of course, is to make friends with someone who keeps
peacocks, for they, like all birds, moult, and the plumes are magnificent.
Budgerigars, the commonest of household pets, cast their small but
vivid feathers, which are well worth saving and much more easily
available.

Many florists' shops and haberdashers sell feathers for decorative
purposes, and there are feather merchants who specialise in supplying
tiny feathers for men's hats, larger ones for women, brightly coloured
feathers for fishing flies, turkey feathers for shuttlecocks, dart flights and
little boys' Red Indian suits. Many of the traditional uses are fading
away as plastic substitutes replace them but in the ever-changing sphere
of fashion they continue to hold their place. Indeed at present, as
feathers are regaining popularity, we seem to be following in the foot-
steps of our Victorian ancestors. Feathers will, I am sure, always be
used for hats, though the shape and size of the Victorian ones demand
a more leisurely pace of life.

Fine feathers can be seen in displays of historic costumes such as at
the Victoria and Albert Museum in South Kensington, London, or
the Bath Costume Museum. A set of cape, hat, muff and scarf made of
peacock feathers individually sewn on by hand can be seen at the
Victoria and Albert Museum. Fans made of ostrich feathers, too, were

Victorian favourites, and sometimes other feathers were added to produce an appliqué decoration to the fan. Goose feathers were often used to make fluffy fans, with fluff added to the feather tips as well as left on at the bottom end. In such a fan at the Victoria and Albert Museum the base of the fan is made of ivory, the join made by inserting the ivory stems into the hollow veins of the feathers. The stem of a feather flower can be extended in the same way. The Victoria and Albert Museum also contains a fine fan made from the feathers of the great argus pheasant, in a natural design, reversed in the centre of the fan to provide variety.

French turban with pheasant tail feathers mounted on net, 1930

The Cecil Beaton exhibition of costume held in London in 1972 included exquisite feather dresses, some of which are illustrated on this page. The methods used in persuading stiff feathers to become pliable, by paring the vein, or frail feathers to become sturdy by means of a backing of net, have been helpful to me in extending techniques for making flowers, and the sight of an entire skirt made of black cockerel hackle feathers an encouraging indication that patience and care in the handling of feathers can be rewarded.

From the minute detail of a doll's hat made of feathers (see page 8) to the extravagance of the feather boa and the theatrical feather fan, Victorians were obsessed with feathers. Whilst the great crested grebe in Britain nearly became extinct as a result of the demand for its thick plumage to make muffs, explorers returned with the exotic skins of the birds of paradise from the Philippines and New Guinea. Like the orchid fever that raised the temperature of the plant hunters, the feather trade crackled into life and many species of bird were trapped and killed for their plumage throughout the nineteenth century, with disastrous results to the rarer species. Legislation in America arrived to end the trade in rare feathers before the end of the century, but it was not until 1921 that Britain passed its Plumage Act, restricting imports to the feathers of certain prescribed species, together with the feathers of birds like turkeys imported for food, and the feathers which formed part of the clothing of travelling ladies. As a result, rare species are today threatened less, whilst the feather collector can still obtain a wide range of colourful feathers within the importation laws.

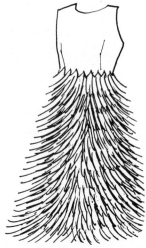

Dress with skirt of cockerel hackles, Givenchy 1968

Though feathers are still used for stuffing pillows, eiderdowns, and even mattresses, a vast quantity of feathers is thrown away or burned when birds are killed for food. An even greater quantity of feathers is shed naturally by birds during moulting. In encouraging the use of feathers for decorative purposes, I am anxious to make clear that the best place for a feather is on the living bird. Any return to the age in which rare and beautiful species were shot for their plumage is happily unthinkable today. The feather collector can find adequate supplies and sources without unnecessary killing or feather farming: what has been discarded is his raw material.

Before becoming embroiled in the feathers themselves and the flowers they make, it is appropriate to make an editorial note, a caveat for all botanists and horticulturalists who read this book. Sometimes it is necessary to give a feather flower a name. Certainly names were

Entire dress dripping with cockerel tails, Givenchy 1960

China picture. The two tiny star flowers (p 47) provide a strong centre, with a periwinkle and three harebells (p 48) pointing out at the corners. The two small globular flowers are duck body feathers pushed, curving inwards, into a piece of *Oasis* attached to a stem. Simple leaves (p 88) made from chicken body feathers are mixed with the flowers. The frame is made of china and stands like a photograph frame.

Coral with flowers. The two main lines in this composition are made by the seven crested pigeon lilies (p   ). The colour of the petals matches that of the piece of natural coral in the centre. The contrasting red protea (p   ) is placed on the point where the lines converge. Six morning glory flowers (p 64) complete the composition, which is arranged in an hors d'oeuvres dish.

Crested Lanterns and Fuchsias. Seven assorted crested lanterns (p 60) are arranged informally, with four fuchsias (p 87) curving over the edge of the vase. The shapes of the two types of flower are complementary. The big simple feathers are grey tail feathers from a sarus crane, contrasting with the seven sprays of loop leaves (p 102). The design is completed with seven simple leaves (p 88).

needed for all the flowers described in this book, to make reference and identification easier. Botanical names have, on the whole, been avoided, for feather flowers, after all, are flights of fancy. However, certain botanical names like lily and daisy have been used, and some generic names like clematis, because such words give an instant general indication of the flower type much more quickly than descriptive circumlocutions. Botanists, therefore, must please refrain from outrage when in the pages that follow a name properly belonging to the natural order of plants is applied to a flower of my imagination.

Goura crested pigeon

2   *Types of Feathers*

When the hoopoe raises his crest or the peacock raises his tail, a really astonishing outgrowth of the animal world is being exhibited. Like the hair on a monkey or a rabbit—or skin itself—feathers provide a protection against the cold, and consist of cells which are fed by the blood supply during their growth but, even at their most glossy and colourful, are dead by the time they reach maturity and their greatest usefulness. For feathers serve functions other than keeping out the cold, and this explains their great variety, which is so important to the feather-flower maker.

They have to resist the pressure of the air when the bird is in flight, and they must be appropriately shaped to help the flow of the air. Those which are concerned with flight have a complex interlocking structure and a distinctive profile. Feathers also help in camouflaging the bird, and in giving important signals in courtship and other purposeful behaviour. They range in colour, therefore, from harmonious natural tones to blend with their surroundings to strident reds and greens which can be displayed to frighten or attract. Finally, they are so layered that often only the tips are visible, and so their pattern varies enormously along their length. The drawings on page 15 show the characteristic basic arrangement, and show how a feather which one may find on the beach or in a cage is not just an anonymous feather but something which can be precisely allocated to one of many different areas of the bird's topography.

The feathers which form the general outline of the body and include

Topography of bird
a outer tail feathers
b upper tail coverts
c scapulars
d back
e nape
f crown
g bend of wing
h wrist
i breast
j wing bars
k primaries
l secondaries
m belly
n wing coverts
o wing linings

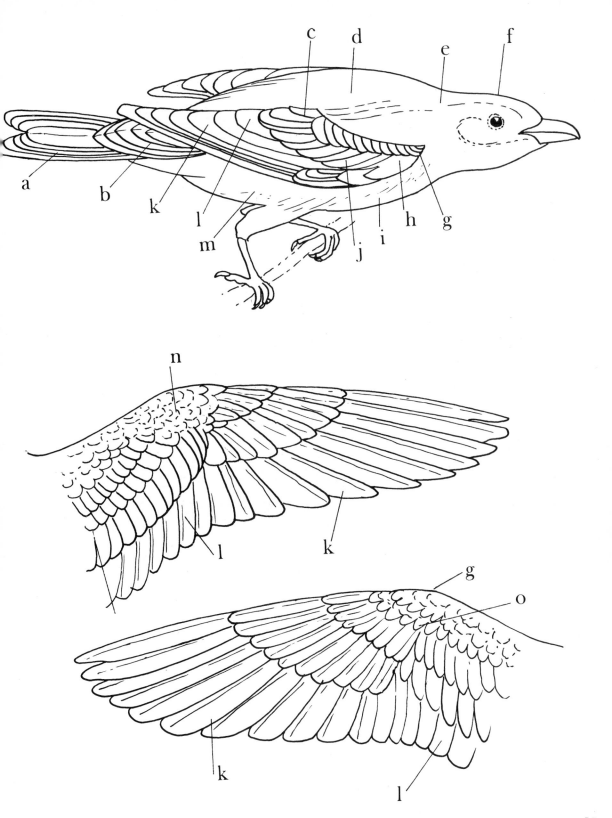

	Bird	Trade name	Position	Group
1	domestic hen	—	wing	2
	domestic hen	—	tail	3
	domestic hen	hackle	neck	2
	domestic hen	—	body	2
2	duck (and drake)	curly tail	tail	4
	duck (and drake)	blue wild	wing	1
	duck (and drake)	light pearl (grey)	body	3
	duck (and drake)	light pearl (black)	body	3
	duck (and drake)	light pearl (brown)	body	3
3	goose	—	wing	1
	goose	cocquille	body	3
	goose	nagoire	shoulder	3
4	partridge, common	—	tail	1
	partridge, common	—	body	3
5	guineafowl	—	wing	1
	guineafowl	—	body	3
6	pheasant, common (cock)	—	tail	1
	pheasant, common (cock)	—	wing	1
	pheasant, common (cock)	red back	body	3
	pheasant, common (cock)	blue back	body	3
	pheasant, common (cock)	red heart	body	3
	pheasant, common (cock)	goldside	body	3
	pheasant, common (cock)	church window	body	3
	pheasant, common (cock)	—	neck	4
	pheasant, common (cock)	cosse	inside wing	2
7	pheasant, common (hen)	—	wing	1
	pheasant, common (hen)	—	body	3
8	pigeon, wood	—	wing	2
	pigeon, wood	—	tail	1
	pigeon, wood	broad, white	wing	2
	pigeon, wood	—	body	3
9	turkey	broad	wing	2
	turkey	spaasem	tail	1
	turkey	marabout	body	3
	turkey	cocquille	body	3

the important flight feathers on the wings are called contour feathers or body feathers, and this category also embraces the strong feathers of the tail. They consist of a central hollow vein or *rhachis* ending in the quill which is embedded in the skin. The vein carries barbs or filaments which are held together by secondary growths or barbules—tiny hooks which prevent the barbs from separating when spread against the wind. The barbs are stronger and harder towards the tip, whilst the quill end has fluffy barbs providing warmth. A cross-section of a primary wing feather will show a gentle S-shaped undulation—not unlike a modern aeroplane wing—to ensure that the feathers interlock, and will also show that the barbs on one side of the vein will be less developed than the other, according to the position of the feather on the bird. These large wing feathers can be paired, however, with their mirror images on the other side of the bird—an important factor for the feather-flower maker, who must often match up feathers of this kind in pairs.

Tail feathers are more symmetrical and blunter, especially those of the super-flyers like the peregrine, but all feathers have a natural curve in the vein, convex on the outer side, as if to enclose and protect the bird. This applies equally to the other major category of feathers—the down feathers, which are soft and fluffy and lie in thick layers beneath the contour feathers. Whilst contour feathers are valuable in making leaves and large bold petals, down feathers are invaluable for the centres of flowers and more delicate petals.

The smallest category of feathers of all—the filo-plumes which grow from the bases of the contour feathers—are not valuable to the feather-flower maker, but the specially adapted contour feathers which occur

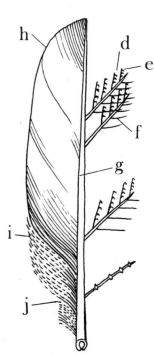

Blood feather

a fine branches forming web (vexillum)
b central shaft (scapus)
c base of shaft

Contour feather

d second order barbs (with humuli)
e first order barbs (contour part)
f second order barbs (without humuli)
g rhachis or vein
h contour part
i fluffy part
j silky part

Feather wheel 1:

	Bird	Trade name	Position	Group	Source
A	budgerigar	—	tail	4	fancier
B	budgerigar	—	body	2	fancier
C	chukka partridge	double barred	wing	3	feather merchant
D	duck	pilet	body	2	feather merchant
E	french partridge	—	wing	3	feather merchant
F	gold and blue macaw	—	wing	4	zoo
G	golden pheasant (cock)	—	collar	3	feather merchant
H	golden pheasant (cock)	greenback	body	3	feather merchant
I	golden pheasant (cock)	red spear	tail	4	feather merchant
J	golden pheasant (cock)	red side	body	3	feather merchant
K	golden pheasant (cock)	gold back	body	3	feather merchant
L	golden pheasant (cock)	blue wing	wing	4	feather merchant
M	golden pheasant (cock)	—	tail	4	feather merchant
N	golden mantled rosella	cocquille	body	3	zoo
O	goose	small nagoire	shoulder	3	feather merchant
P	goose	sattin	underwing	2	florist
Q	goose	nagoire	shoulder	3	feather merchant
R	goose	biot	wing	4	feather merchant
S	goura crested pigeon	—	crest	4	feather merchant

in tails (think of cockerels, pheasants' tails up to 70in long, the curly tail feathers of the mallard drake, peacocks' tails) and in crests (the crested pigeon) are particularly valuable in making the centres and dominant features of spectacular flowers. See page 56.

The texture of feathers varies enormously according to the type, and from bird to bird. Ostrich feathers, familiarly floppy and frond-like, suffice for the ostrich because it no longer tries to fly. They would not support it if it did, for though they are contour feathers the barbs bear no hooks to hold them together and the filaments fall apart. The owl is a bird with particularly soft feathers, often beautifully marked. Water birds like geese and ducks have vast quantities of soft feathers for protection from the cold, as conscientious pluckers know only too well, and one hardly needs reminding of the comforting qualities of eider down. Some species, however, have coarse, hard plumage, especially tropical birds like the parrot, whilst the penguin in any icy climate grows specially adapted plumage not unlike fur. Fortunately for the feather-flower maker, a comprehensive range of feathers comes from the birds which are reared for food. Goose feathers—mainly plain coloured—and pheasant feathers—exotic and varied, with a wide range of patterns—provide between them most of the flower-making feathers.

Feathers plucked from the bird are easy to classify. It is quite another matter when sorting out a sack from a poulterer or a chest of feathers from the attic. Correct topographical definitions or simple classification on the basis of size fall short when one enters the specialised world of the feather merchant, who sells pilets, nagoires, sattins, hackles and biots and, with the precision of a jeweller, divides pheasant feathers into church windows, red hearts, gold sides and red spears.

In order to identify the precise feathers used in making the flowers in chapter 4, these trade names are used, and an identification key provided with the drawings on pages 19 and 20. The feathers readily available from the poulterer and butcher are shown in the photograph on page 17, again with a key.

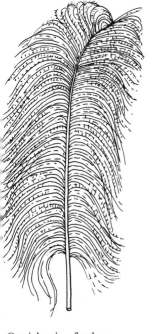

Ostrich wing feather

Feather wheel 2:

	Bird	Trade name	Position	Group	Source
A	great bustard	—	wing	4	florist
B	jungle cock	hackle, striped	neck	2	feather merchant
C	jungle cock	hackle, speckled	neck	2	feather merchant
D	jungle cock	hackle, white	breast	2	feather merchant
E	jungle cock	bronze	tail	1	feather merchant
F	military macaw	—	body	3	zoo
G	military macaw	—	wing	4	zoo
H	ostrich	—	body	3	florist
I	peacock	—	body	3	zoo
J	rhea	—	wing	4	florist
K	sarus crane	—	wing	4	zoo
L	teal	—	breast	3	feather merchant
M	white peacock	—	tail	4	zoo

To assist the flower maker in the sorting and storing of these feathers, I have divided them into groups indicated in the keys, based on size and use.

Group 1 contains the very large feathers which are more suitable for use on their own, much as one would use ferns and leaves as a background in a flower arrangement. Their barbs are readily cut to shape.

Group 2 contains the stiff contour feathers for use individually or as petals. The strong vein makes feathers of this group suitable for the flat petals of the daisy family, as they can be difficult to curve and may need shaving to weaken the vein. Their barbs can easily be cut to shape.

Group 3 is the largest group, consisting of soft down feathers, for use as petals and centres.

Group 4 contains the special feathers, which are least numerous and most beautiful—the stars of the show.

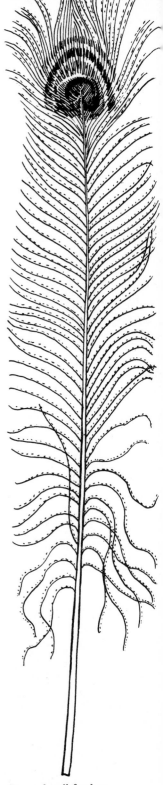

Peacock tail feather

3 *The Raw Materials: Preparing the Feathers*

Prepared feathers

The basic similarity between the shape of a feather and that of a leaf or a petal is striking. From the petals of a common daisy in the lawn to the more exotic petals of a cyclamen in the house or the bold leaves of a rubber plant, this concordance of shape is confirmed again and again, and for the flower maker it is a great help: it not only saves time, but also helps to make the finished result look natural.

There is no point, however, in copying nature with fine botanical detail, for feather flowers are made for decoration, not fertilisation, and the decorative quality must always be the first consideration.

The feathers detailed in chapter 2 will serve to make leaves—all feathers, like leaves, have a central vein and a springy curve—petals, stamens, and in some cases the calyx. For stalks and the pistil at the centre of the flower one has to look to other materials, either artificial or natural.

Dried seed heads on their stems, small fir cones, teazels, and grasses are useful as centres for feather flowers, and a full list with illustrations is given on page 28. The teazel is a particularly useful natural starting point for not only is its many-celled head a good anchorage for feathers to make the centre of the flower, but its stem is usually resilient enough to support the finished bloom. In most cases the stem for feather flowers, for leaves and for some petals has to be made from wire. Florists' wire or stem wire is the best material. It is strong but it puts up no resistance when it is bent, and once bent or curved to an angle will stay that way. Feather-flower makers should equip themselves with bundles of stem

Natural curves of a feather

23

wires, which are very cheap and available in several lengths. Another kind of wire, much finer and comparable to 15 amp fuse wire, is needed to attach feathers to their stems. It is referred to as binding wire and can be bought from florists as well as electrical and hardware stores. The other material for holding parts of the flower together is glue, and the quicker-setting the better. UHU or balsa cement are the best and have the advantage of being nearly invisible when dry.

If natural materials like seed heads are unsuitable for the centres of the flowers, there are two light-weight, inert and entirely appropriate materials which come to our aid. *Oasis*, a branded plastic foam available from florists, comes in green coloured blocks which are easy to cut, and will obligingly grip the feather stems which are pushed into it. *Styrofoam* balls, available in several sizes, have similar properties and are useful for flower centres because of their spherical shape. These artificial centres are often hidden from sight by a covering of small feathers.

Feathers themselves can be used to make the stamens, though they are not always suitable, and an assortment of beads will be useful here. Glass drops, pearls, wooden beads and coloured beads in different sizes, can be threaded onto wires to make pendant or protruding stamens in such flowers as fuchsias (p 87) or snowdrops (p 44), or compact centres of such flowers as the bead daisy (p 69) or spherical centres of such flowers as the arrow flower (p 85).

The only other material needed is a binding material to cover joints and give some naturalism to the stems. Gutta percha, a florists' tape made specially for covering stems, is the best. It is slightly stretchy and has the special quality of being adhesive only to itself. Made in natural shades of green, white and brown, it can be used to simulate the calyx of the flower and to cover all leaf and flower stems. Crêpe paper will do as a substitute—it is sometimes preferable if bright colours are required—and should be cut across the roll into strips about $\frac{1}{2}$in wide. In the instructions in chapters 4 and 5, gutta percha is always quoted, but crêpe paper can be substituted in every case.

The flower maker should also be equipped with scissors, wire cutters, pins and a knife, and is then ready to start.

Feathers are very special things to work with. They have their own characteristics and limitations which must be respected if successful flowers are to be made. Every feather has a curve of its own, which can be increased or altered by artificial means, but for the beginner it is best to choose a flower such as a simple daisy (p 30) which can be made from feathers in their natural state, without any treatment. Handling can easily damage feathers, and should be kept to a minimum.

Any feather can be trimmed with scissors to alter its shape, and some of the barbs can be removed by stripping them from the centre vein. The fluff near the base of the feathers can be stripped off, leaving a cleaner shape, and also greater unity of colour, for the fluff is often a neutral colour which contrasts with the contour part of the feather.

The central vein of most feathers can be made more curved by running it between the thumb and a scissor blade or sharp knife. The amount of pressure needed will be a matter for experiment, and will

Feather curved over scissor blade

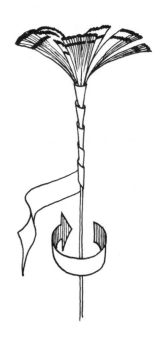

Binding a stem

shave back off vein

Dip-dyed feather

depend on the type of feather used. Some flight feathers have such strong centre veins that the hard pressure required will kink the vein in several places and destroy its curve. The solution to this problem is to shave the back of the vein down with a razor blade. It is a tricky thing to do, as the barbs are easily cut by the blade, and the best way to go about it is to lay the feather face down over a convex surface, so that it is curving against its natural shape and the vein is prominent. If an even layer of the vein is cut away, the feather becomes more manageable—rather floppy in fact—and easy to curve with a scissor blade.

If your feathers begin to show the signs of too much handling, they can soon be restored by holding them in the steam from a kettle for about half a minute. By the time they have dried their barbs can be stroked back into place; this is an excellent tonic for restoring fluffy feathers such as ostrich and turkey marabout.

In view of the delicate and subtle colouring of natural feathers, it seems incredible that one should sometimes want to change them, but dyeing feathers can help to complete a colour scheme, and when boiled in a fabric dye, feathers colour extremely well. They can be dried easily with a fan heater, and their shape and character restored by holding them in steam *after* they are dry. Interesting effects can be made if one part of the feather is dyed, such as the tip (useful when making daisy petals), or if one side of the leaf is dyed up to the vein, for making bi-coloured leaves (p 89). They can also be dyed twice, once to change the colour of the whole, and the second time, by dipping, to concentrate or contrast the colour of the tip.

Another method of colouring is by painting, and although spray painting, particularly with metallic colours, can be effective for Christmas feather flowers, the disadvantage of the method is that it stiffens the feathers and makes further manipulation difficult. Spray paints are perhaps best used to colour completed flowers.

The normal sequence of making the flower starts with the centre. If this is not to consist of a natural material such as a dried seed head, it will mean joining either beads or feathers to a stem wire. The size of the feathers used for the centre must relate to the size of the petals, and it is a good general rule to choose feathers of approximately the same length for each. Long thin feathers such as biots can be made to curl by running them against a scissor blade, and if long pheasant tail feathers are stripped of their barbs completely down one side, they can be curled into attractive spirals by the same method. Being somewhat floppy, both of these types make good stamens for a flower which hangs its head, such as the sun lily (p 83). Exotic crest feathers, precious and hard to obtain, make magnificent stamens as in the frosted pine lily (p 75). Delicate projecting stamens can be made from pheasant and partridge body feathers stripped completely of their barbs except for the very tip, as in the periwinkle (p 35). The stamens should always be grouped together, their number varying from flower to flower, and attached to a stem wire with binding wire. Where stamens are made from artificial materials such as the cherries used in the poppy (p 55), they will be attached first to a *Styrofoam* ball, or a piece of *Oasis*. These

Wired feather curved backwards

materials are also necessary for global and hemispherical centres of such flowers as the umbrella flower (p 45) and the tropical lily (p 82). A global centre consisting of a *Styrofoam* ball is usually concealed by a covering of feathers pushed into the surface (see p 50) or glued over it in a mosaic (see p 45), or it can be closely studded with beads threaded onto pins and pushed into the ball (see p 69). Such complex centres are often turned into effective flowers by surrounding them with simple petals.

Finally, a centre can be made with a single 'stamen' or 'stigma' consisting of a bead (see p 59). The shape and normally shiny surface of the bead makes an excellent contrast to the feather petals, and as a focus of attention can create the whole character of the flower—see morning glory (p 64). Such a centre is made from a pearl already attached to a wire pin, but can be made by threading the wire through a bead and twisting the wire back on itself.

The petals of many flowers are made simply by arranging feathers carefully in position around the centre and fixing them with wire and glue. Instructions for individual flowers are given in chapter 4. The vein of the feather may have to be kinked at the binding point to give the petal the correct angle, or it may need the aid of a stem wire. If a covered wire is glued to the vein of the feather it can be curved to take up whatever angle is necessary, though the tip of the feather—where the strain is greatest—will tend to break away from the wire, and must be securely glued. If a feather is wired and bent *against* its natural curve the unusual petals of irises and parrot tulips can be suggested (pp 59 and 61).

An entirely new range of shapes and textures is created if feathers are combined with paper or card mounts to make both petals and leaves. Some of the natural qualities of the feathers, such as translucency, are lost, but there are other advantages—composite petals can be made from several small feathers, and the delicate outline of fine feathers like the pigeon breasts can be contrasted with an artificial backing. Both acetate (for contrast) and netting (for a nearly invisible support) are useful materials for mounting. Examples of mounted petals can be seen in the ice flower (p 49) and the peacock flower (p 81).

Mounting and the preparation of composite petals and leaves can lead to very intricate patterns and colour schemes, and a three-dimensional petal can be made by glueing a biot vertically along the length of the central vein. One rule, however, in controlling these patterned petals is that the parts must always appear to have grown naturally from the stem, otherwise the fantasy flies too far from nature and the result is a muddle.

Composition in natural shades. Most of this arrangement consists of dried flowers —protea seed head, lotus seed head, two bulrushes, five verbascum seeds and nine magnolia skeleton leaves. In the centre are three bead daisies (p 69).

27

When the flower head is complete, the base of the petals should be bound as tightly as possible with gutta percha, to make the calyx, squeezing the binding between the thumb and forefinger of the right hand. Binding the rest of the stem then comes easily—simply roll the stem between thumb and forefinger, whilst holding the roll of tape in tension with the other hand. If the tape is held at an angle to the stem, it will cover it with a neat spiral.

Similar flowers or leaves can be added to the stem or made separately. Now is the time to try for yourself.

Dried plants:
Left to right: bells of Ireland, bulrush, fir cone, hare's-tail grass, honesty, lotus seed head, protea seed head, rush, skeleton fern, skeleton magnolia leaf, teazel, verbascum

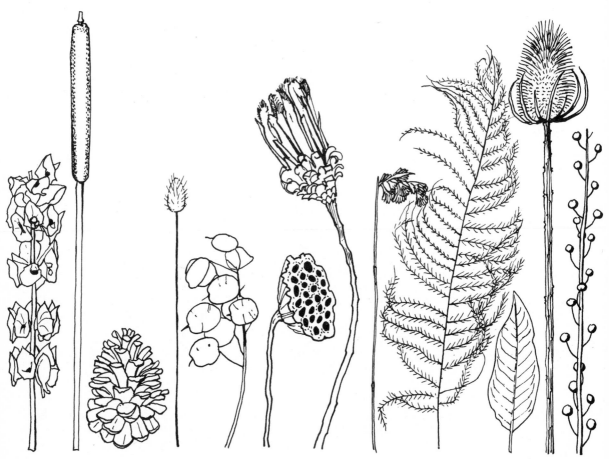

Feathers and ferns. The two arrow flowers (p 85) give a horizontal emphasis to this composition. The feather petals have been dyed to match the dark turquoise beads chosen, like the dark green pheasant feathers in the umbrella flower (p 45), and to contrast with the creamy colours of the natural materials. These are three bells of Ireland and five skeleton ferns. The seven striped feathers are from a great bustard.

4 *Making the Flowers*

Simple Daisy

Feathers
6 turkey sattins, 5in long
Other materials
puff ball
1 stem wire
gutta percha and glue

Centre
The puff ball forms the centre of this daisy. It can be dyed or used in its natural white colour. Glue it to the top of the stem wire and cover the stem with gutta percha, Fig 1.
Petals
Dye the feathers if required. Cut the feathers to a simple pointed shape, removing all the fluff, Fig 2, and make all six petals uniform in size.
Assembly
Apply glue to the lower half of the puff ball, that is the part nearest the stem. Attach the petals so that they touch each other as they radiate in a flat plane around the centre.

A wooden bead can be used to replace the puff ball in the centre. This can be of any size, and the size governs the size to which the petals should be cut. Choose flat feathers for the petals so that the flat profile is not broken up. If the feathers are used in their natural state, giving the petals a rounded end, a useful variation can be achieved. This flower is effective with patterned dyeing, by dipping twice or painting part of each petal, or spraying parts of each feather, allowing dots of paint to fall on the rest. The puff ball can also be sprayed. The rather flat and hard appearance of this daisy contrasts well with fluffy flowers and leaves in an arrangement.

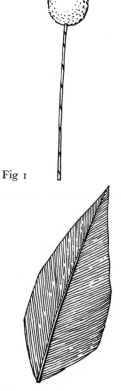

Fig 1

Fig 2

Curly Wig Flower

Feathers
Approximately 30 ostrich body feathers,
 4in long
Other materials
Oasis ball
3 stem wires
gutta percha and glue

Centre
Cover all three stem wires together with gutta percha, apply glue to the top and push into the ball of *Oasis*, Fig 1.

Petals
Curve all the feathers over a scissor blade. When the centre vein has been curved, the bracts will follow the shape, Fig 2.

Assembly
Start three-quarters of the way down the ball and push the curved feathers into it *in pairs* with a little glue, Fig 3. They should all curve outwards, but at different angles, so that they appear to intermingle. Continue adding the feathers until the centre is reached and a globe is completed.

This big curly flower is suitable for modern arrangements, but also looks well in a bunch with dried plants. As the feathers are used in pairs an interesting effect can be achieved by using two shades; try making a flower with feathers of two colours, and then a second one with the same colours, but with the order of the feathers reversed.

Fig 1

Fig 2

Fig 3

Goose Lily

Feathers
5 goose nagoires, 6in long
Other materials
9 pearl beads
4 stem wires
gutta percha
binding wire

Centre
Cover the top inch of each of the three stem wires with gutta percha. Then thread three beads onto each and cover the remainder of the wire with gutta percha. Bunch the three together, avoiding an even grouping, and bind them together with binding wire, adding the other stem wire at this stage, Fig 1.

Petals
Dye the feathers to the required shade. Trim them to a simple pointed shape, removing the fluff, Fig 2.

Assembly
Arrange the five feathers around the centre. Bind tightly with binding wire, then cover the base of the petals and stem with gutta percha.

The goose lily is a versatile flower, equally effective when used upright or hanging down. The very simple shape makes it an easy flower to use. Several blooms in a large formal arrangement will make an explosive profusion of flowers. It has a good profile and can be used effectively at the edge of a composition. All goose feathers, from nagoires to cocquilles, can be used for this flower, giving variations of size. This is an easy flower for the beginner.

Fig 1

Fig 2

Spray of Hops

Feathers
40 goose cocquilles, 3in long
Other materials
5 puff balls
5 stem wires
gutta percha and glue

Centre
Dye the puff balls and the feathers together if required. Glue each puff ball onto the top of a stem wire, covering the stems with gutta percha, Fig 1.
Petals
The feathers, dyed or self-coloured, are used in their natural state with their fluff on.
Assembly
Apply glue all over one of the puff balls. Put four feathers, curved inwards, at equal distances around the sides of the ball with the base of the veins pointing towards the stem, Fig 2. Arrange and attach four more feathers in the spaces between the others; it may be necessary to add more glue for this second layer. Repeat this with the other four puff balls. Build up the spray shape of the finished form by arranging them in a bunch with stems of different lengths and binding them all together with gutta percha.

The hops should be globular in shape. A difficulty in making flowers from fluffy feathers by gluing rather than wiring is that the feathers tend to stick only by the fluff. Using the right amount of glue is crucial; too much soaks right through the surface and produces shiny patches or worse. Hops can of course be made with any number of heads, and large sprays are more useful for the larger, more elaborate arrangements.

Fig 1

Fig 2

Periwinkle

Feathers
7 pigeon wing feathers, 3½in long
3 pheasant red hearts, 3in long
Other materials
knapweed seed head
glue

Centre
Dry the knapweed until the seed head opens flat, Fig 1. Strip the pheasant feathers to within ½in of the tip, taking care not to damage the vein. The tip will appear to be on a long stem. Cut these stems to three different lengths.

Petals
Trim the pigeon feathers to a pointed shape, Fig 2.

Assembly
Glue the three pheasant stems together in a bunch. Glue the pigeon feathers, with the curve outwards, to the *top* surface of the seed head, with their bases touching in the centre, arranging them evenly in the circle, Fig 3. Glue the bunch of tips into the centre. To ensure adhesion these have to be held until the glue is dry enough to keep them upright.

There are many feathers which make good substitutes for the pigeon as long as there is enough fluff and they can be cut to a tip. Peacock body feathers make an exotic alternative centre.

Fig 1

Fig 2

Fig 3

Basket of Flowers. The flowers are standing in a block of *Oasis*, which is wired inside a wooden trug. Six peacock tail feathers around the edge set the colour scheme for this arrangement in purple, green, blue and white. Two clematis (p 67) are made in shades of purple. Iridescent feathers are used for the globular flowers around the central large green begonia (p 77). Three tulip marabouts (p 41) and white mimosa leaves (p 104) help to lighten the arrangement, which was designed for an unlit corner.

34

Rose

Feathers
many pheasant church windows, tips
Other materials
dried teazel (Fig 1)
glue

Petals
Cut all the feathers to leave tips of approximately 1in, Fig 2.
Assembly
Start at the top of the teazel head and push some of the glued feathers, curved inwards, between the scales to form a tight circle, Fig 3. Add another circle just below the first, then another and continue until the whole head is hidden. Every feather will need glue at its base but it is best to glue these as they are required, to prevent them from drying out before use. The teazel stem can be left uncovered as a support for the flower.

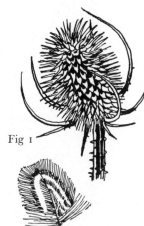

Fig 1

The feathers should be chosen for their pattern, because plain feathers tend to soften the image and so produce a flower which looks like a fluffy ball. Pheasant red hearts and partridge feathers are alternatives which have appropriate patterns.

Fig 2

Fig 3

Spider Flower

Feathers
many turkey cocquilles, 3in long
approximately 24 cockerel hackles
Other materials
half a ball of *Oasis*
3 stem wires
gutta percha and glue

Centre
Push the three stem wires separately into the back, flat side of the *Oasis* and then bind them together with gutta percha. Using the turkey cocquilles curving inwards, push one into the centre of the *Oasis* with a little glue, and continue adding them one by one until the whole dome is covered, Fig 1.
Petals
The cockerel hackles are used in their natural state, Fig 2.
Assembly
Push the hackles, curving outwards, into the edge of the *Oasis* with a little glue, just behind the dome of cocquilles, making a complete circle.

One or two of these large wispy flowers very quickly make their presence felt in an arrangement.

Fig 1

Fig 2

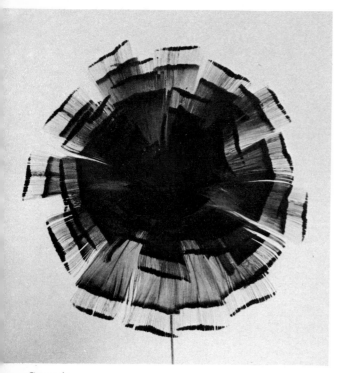

Carnation

Silver primrose

Crested lantern

Fuchsia

ce flower

Rose

ropical lily

Cactus flower

Globe Flower

Feathers
15 breast feathers
Other materials
1 puff ball
1 stem wire
gutta percha and glue

Centre
Cover the stem wire with gutta percha, apply glue to the top and push it into the puff ball, Fig 1.
Petals
The little breast feathers are used in their natural state, but with a little of the fluff removed, Fig 2.
Assembly
Apply glue to the entire surface of the puff ball. Place three of the feathers so that they overlap in the centre, like the heart of a cabbage. Continue attaching feathers individually, allowing the tips to overlap the bases of the feathers above. Because of the round shape of the ball, the tips will stand free and should be arranged as closely as is necessary to make a dense cluster of petals.

There are many sizes of puff ball, the larger ones of which could be used for a base for large feathers. Body feathers are, however, the most suitable because their strong curve keeps the whole flower held in a tight ball shape.

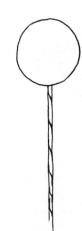

Fig 1

Fig 2

Hollyhock

Feathers
36 golden pheasant collars, about 3in long
Other materials
1 long stem wire
2 short stem wires
binding wire
gutta percha

Centre
It is not really necessary to give centres to these flowers, but single beads can be used if required.
Petals
The feathers are likely to vary in size slightly, so arrange them in three groups according to size. Each feather should be curved slightly at the base, Fig 1.
Assembly
Arrange one group of feathers round one of the short stem wires and bind tightly with binding wire. The feathers should just touch each other to make a conical shape with no gaps. Cover the base of the petals and stem with gutta percha, Fig 2. Repeat this with the other two groups, using the long stem wire and the remaining short one. Attach one of the short-stemmed flowers to the stem of the long-stemmed flower, about 4in below the flower head, using gutta percha to hold them together. Then add the third in the same way. Bend the stem of each flower just below the base of the petals so that the flower faces outwards, and arrange the two lower flowers so that they face alternate sides.

Columns of hollyhocks can be made with the addition of any number of flower heads. Double hollyhocks can be made by using many more feathers in two or even three layers of petals. Where collar feathers are not available, a fan-shaped feather is a possible substitute. Tips of turkey tail feathers (for big hollyhocks) or double-bar partridge feathers can be used. In an arrangement, the hollyhocks look best when erect, as they grow in the garden.

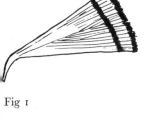

Fig 1

Fig 2

Tulip Marabout

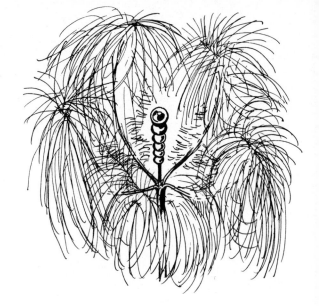

Feathers
5 turkey marabout, 5in long
Other materials
6 beads
6 stem wires
binding wire
gutta percha and glue

Centre
Thread one stem wire with six beads. Secure them with glue at the top and cover the remainder of the wire with gutta percha, Fig 1.

Petals
Cover the other five wires with gutta percha. Glue one to the back of the vein of each feather, Fig 2.

Assembly
Arrange the petals around the centre with the curves inwards, and bind tightly with wire. Cover the whole stem. Bend all the petals out from the centre and then curve them in at the top—see the drawing of the finished shape.

Several of these tulips, wired together, make a useful spray for the larger arrangement. Tulip marabouts seem to come to life when placed in a draught, when the bloom will quiver attractively. Flat feathers should be chosen for the leaves to accompany these fluffy flowers.

Fig 1

Fig 2

Cherry Flower

Feathers
7 teal breast feathers
6 red hearts
Other materials
1 small puff ball
1 stem wire
binding wire
gutta percha and glue

Centre
Cover the stem wire with gutta percha, apply glue to the top and push it into the puff ball. Apply glue all over the surface of the puff ball and press on the base of the teal feathers, allowing the tips to curve over the ball and so follow its shape, Fig 1.

Petals
The red hearts are used in their natural state, with all their fluff retained, Fig 2.

Assembly
Arrange the petals, curved outwards, around the stem below the centre and bind tightly with binding wire. If these are bound very closely under the centre, they will be held in place and at the right angle by the puff ball.

This small flower can be made from a whole host of body feathers. Combinations of pigeon and duck, chicken and pheasant or partridge and goose feathers all help to make these charming little flowers valuable for miniature arrangements.

Fig 1

Fig 2

Snowdrop

Feathers
6 goose cocquilles, 4in long
Other materials
6 glass drop beads
binding wire
stem wire
gutta percha

Centre
Cut six pieces of binding wire of varying lengths. Thread a bead on each, securing each one by twisting the wire back on itself. Arrange them in a bunch and bind tightly to the stem wire, Fig 1.
Petals
Use the feathers in their natural state, with their fluff removed, but dyed if necessary, Fig 2.
Assembly
Arrange the petals, curving inwards, around the centre and bind tightly with binding wire. If the tips of the petals touch at the centre bend each petal outwards slightly at the point where it is bound. Cover the base of the petals and stem with gutta percha. Curve the whole stem over gently but progressively so that the flower head is held like its natural counterpart.

This delicate little flower can be used to lighten a rather solid arrangement, particularly when allowed to overhang the vase. A double snowdrop can be made by assembling two layers of petals, possibly of contrasting colours. The delicate quality of this little flower is enhanced by the glass beads in the centre, so give them adequate stems and make sure that they are not completely hidden by the petals.

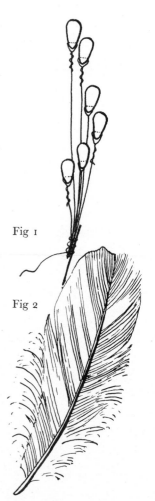

Fig 1

Fig 2

Umbrella Flower

Feathers
approximately 24 golden pheasant neck
    feathers
12 golden pheasant back feathers (gold)
12 golden pheasant back feathers (green)
Other materials
Half an *Oasis* ball
3 stem wires
gutta percha and glue

Fig 1

Centre
Bind the three stems together with gutta percha, apply glue to the top
and push it into the flat side of the *Oasis* ball. Cover the whole of the
dome with glue. Arrange the tiny neck feathers on the dome, starting
in the centre, to form a scale sequence over the entire surface, Fig 1.

Petals
Both kinds of feathers should be used in the natural state with the fluff
retained, Fig 2.

Assembly
Push the gold petals, curving outwards, into the *Oasis* with a little glue.
Place the green ones just under the gold. If the feathers are pushed in
parallel to the flat side of the *Oasis* ball, their natural curve will give
the flower its umbrella shape.

A highly patterned flower like this can usefully be contrasted with
simple flowers in an arrangement. It demonstrates how minute feathers
applied to a dome surface can make an intricate and attractive centre.

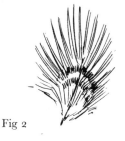

Fig 2

Fig 3

Star Flower

Feathers
5 turkey tail feathers, broads, full length
Other materials
6 wooden beads
1 stem wire
binding wire
gutta percha

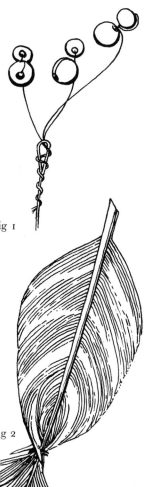

g 1

g 2

Centre
The wooden beads are used for the centre in natural colours or dyed. Cut three different lengths of binding wire and thread two beads on each. Twist each one to secure the beads at the top. Bunch these together and bind them to the top of the stem wire with binding wire, Fig 1.

Petals
The five turkey feathers are to be used with their tips towards the centre of the flower. The widest parts of the feathers should be chosen and 6in lengths cut from each. Taking one length, for an inch on each side peel away the barbs from the lower end. Squeeze the feather to a point at the opposite end—the tip—and bind it tightly with wire, Fig 2. Keep the barbs carefully together. Repeat this with the other four feathers.

Assembly
Arrange the petals, curving outwards, around the centre and bind them tightly. Finally cover the base of the petals and stem with gutta percha. Should the single stem wire be too flimsy to support the flower head, one or two more can be added and bound.

White or black turkey feathers are equally suitable for star flowers. An arrangement using both black and white flowers can look most effective.

Glass Dome. A Victorian glass dome 12in high contains and protects the flowers in this arrangement, made from the bright plumage of a tropical bird, the golden-mantled rossela. It consists of four globe flowers (p 40), twelve dewdrop flowers (p 62) with glass bead centres, and three jonquils (p 52) at the top. Clear blue wing feathers are placed in a rosette of leaves around the bottom of the arrangement.

47

Harebell

Feathers
5 pheasant neck feathers
3 ostrich barbs
Other materials
hare's-tail grass
Stem wire
binding wire
gutta percha and glue

Centre
The hare's-tail grass forms the centre. Wire the stem of the grass to the stem wire and cover both with gutta percha. Curl the three ostrich barbs over a scissor blade. Holding them in a bunch, put some glue on the base of the barbs and push them into the top of the hare's-tail grass, Fig 1.

Petals
The five little pheasant feathers are used in their natural form, Fig 2.

Assembly
Glue the feathers, curved inwards, into the side of the hare's-tail grass halfway down, so that they encircle the grass and end by touching each other. Curve the whole stem over so that the flower hangs down.

True harebells do not have long curling stamens, but the curly ostrich barbs used here add zest to the shape. A flower of this small size provides opportunity to use many of the really tiny feathers, which one might otherwise discard.

Fig 1

Fig 2

48

Ice Flower

Feathers
many pigeon body feathers, 2in long
6 pheasant wing feathers
Other materials
1 large pearl bead
cartridge paper
7 stem wires
gutta percha and glue

Centre
Put some glue onto the top of a stem wire and insert it into the bead. Cover the stem with gutta percha, Fig 1.

Petals
These are mounted petals, so first cut six simple pointed petal shapes out of the cartridge paper a little larger all round than the pheasant wing feathers, Fig 2. Run a line of glue up the centre of each one and attach a wire. This is the surface onto which the feathers will be glued. Apply glue all round the edge of the petal shape to the width of about an inch. Glue on the pigeon body feathers, radiating from the base of the petal and overlapping the edge of the mount, Fig 3. Fill the centre with glue and place a pheasant wing feather in the space. Repeat this mounting pattern with the other five petals. Bend all the stem wires back at the base of the petals.

Assembly
Arrange the petals around the centre and bind the whole bunch of stems with gutta percha.

This ice flower is, of course, entirely fantasy, but it is usefully made from small feathers readily obtained from a poulterer. The exotic design contrasts well with some of the more plain and simple flowers, and the three-dimensional effect given by the pigeon feathers is shown to advantage when the flower is lit from the side.

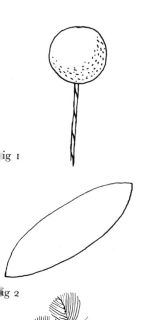

Fig 1

Fig 2

Fig 3

49

Snowball

Feathers
approximately 15 grey goose nagoires,
4in long
6 grey goose cocquilles, 2in long
Other materials
Oasis ball
3 stem wires
gutta percha and glue

Centre
The *Oasis* forms the centre of the snowball. Cover all three stem wires together with gutta percha, apply glue to the top and push it into the *Oasis* ball.
Petals
Both types of feather are used in their natural state with all the fluff retained, Fig 1.
Assembly
Push the cocquilles, curving inwards, into the centre of the *Oasis* with a little glue. They should form a small dome shape in the middle, Fig 2. Add the nagoires separately in similar fashion. Care should be taken with the angle: the feathers should be pushed in to achieve a ball shape.

This is a big flower for large arrangements. Goose feathers have just the right amount of curve to form a snowball; in using other feathers for this design remember that the size of the ball will be governed by the amount of curve in the feathers.

Fig 1

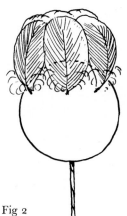

Fig 2

Giant Daisy

Feathers
many white pigeon wing feathers,
4in long
many brown mallard breast feathers
Other materials
half a ball of *Oasis*
3 stem wires
gutta percha

Centre
Push all the stem wires into the flat side of the *Oasis* ball, keeping them slightly apart at their tips, but bound together with gutta percha. This makes for a more stable form and prevents the flower head from twisting round. Starting in the centre of the hemisphere, push in the mallard feathers so that they point together at the centre. Go on adding them one by one until the whole surface of the *Oasis* is covered and the feathers have formed a solid dome, Fig 1.

Petals
Dip the tip of each feather separately into a strong dye, one that will contrast well with the main colour. The feathers are otherwise used in their natural state with their fluff on. Try to select matching feathers, if possible from the same side of the bird.

Assembly
Push the pigeon feathers all around the perimeter of the *Oasis*. Each feather should just touch its neighbour and lie directly behind the mallard-feather 'dome'.

This easily-recognisable shape is useful in an arrangement with fluffy flowers. Different and more complicated designs can be made by dip-dyeing the same feathers several times, each time dipping the feathers in to different levels. The small flat feathers from the pigeon are particularly effective, and if a substitute is used it must have the same form.

Fig 1

Jonquil

Feathers
5 breast feathers
Other materials
5 glass bagette beads
1 stem wire
binding wire
gutta percha

Centre
Cut five pieces of binding wire, one a little longer than the others. Thread a bead onto each wire and twist the end back on itself to secure the bead. Arrange them into a bunch with the long one in the centre and bind them together to the top of the stem wire, Fig 1.
Petals
Small breast feathers are used in their natural state with all their fluff retained, Fig 2.
Assembly
Arrange the five small feathers, curving outwards, around the centre. Cover the base of the feathers and stem with gutta percha and bend the stem over just below the flower head so that the flower is held at an angle.

This tiny flower was used in the glass dome in the arrangement on p 46, where size was a limiting factor. The size of the beads chosen for the centre will govern the size of the feathers used for the petals, and so the flower is quite adaptable.

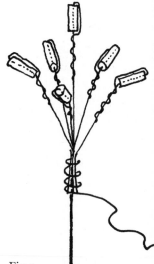

Fig 1

Fig 2

White Poppies. Big white poppies (p 55) are arranged informally with bulrushes (p 97). Branches of bracken (p 110) curve down from the centre. Apart from peacock feathers at the back, the arrangement consists entirely of chicken, turkey and duck feathers.

Mallow

Feathers
9 pigeon body feathers, 3in long
5 pheasant church windows, tips
Other materials
knapweed seed head
glue

Centre
Dry the knapweed seed head until it opens out flat to form the surface onto which the petals are to be glued, Fig 1.
Petals
The pigeon feathers are used whole. Cut the tips from the pheasant feathers.
Assembly
Glue the pigeon feathers onto the knapweed with the curve outwards, so that the bases touch in the centre and the tips spread out evenly all round, Fig 2. The tips of the pheasant feathers are glued into the centre to make a pattern covering the base of the pigeon feathers.

Fig 1

The mallow can be made with other small feathers with the fluff retained. Plain feathers should be used to replace the pigeon feathers so that a contrast can be made with the brightly coloured feathers of the central pattern. For an even brighter effect one or both parts of the flower can be dyed. Being a small, delicate type of flower, this is suitable for small arrangements or a large display when made into sprays or branches.

Fig 2

Poppy

Feathers
8 turkey cocquilles, 3in long
Other materials
1 *Styrofoam* ball
8 imitation holly berries
1 imitation cherry
stem wire
gutta percha and glue

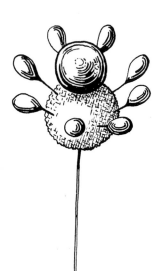

Centre
The *Styrofoam* ball is the true centre. Cover the stem wire with gutta percha, put a little glue on the top and push it into the foam ball. Push the cherry into the centre, followed by the holly berries, placing them so that they encircle the cherry, Fig 1.
Petals
To contrast with the bright red berries, the turkey feathers are left white and used in their natural state.
Assembly
Push the turkey feathers, curved inwards, into the ball. Each feather should just touch its neighbour.

Several of these in a vase look like big white cups, their bright centres adding an extra detail. *Oasis* cut to shape can be a substitute for the *Styrofoam*. Pearl beads could be used instead of berries, in which case the feathers can be dyed to improve the colour scheme.

Fig 1

Crested Pigeon Lily

Feathers
4 crest feathers, various sizes
5 pheasant gold sides, 4in long
Other materials
1 stem wire
binding wire
gutta percha

Centre
Make a bunch of the crest feathers and bind them tightly to the stem wire, Fig 1.
Petals
The gold sides are used in their natural state with the fluff retained, Fig 2.
Assembly
Arrange the feathers, curving outwards, around the centre and bind them tightly with binding wire. Cover the base of the petals and stem with gutta percha. Bend the stem over below the base of the petals so that the flower faces to the side.

The crest feathers, the 'stamens', are the most attractive feature of this flower, and they move in the slightest current of air. With goose feathers as petals, the centres can be made from peacock barbs or grasses. Pheasant red spears also make excellent centres and can be attractive combined with church windows as petals.

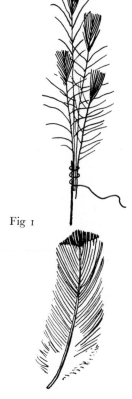

Fig 1

Fig 2

Flowers in an Italian Urn. All the feathers in this arrangement come from the pigeon and the pheasant. In the centre are two periwinkles (p 34) and five mallows (p 54). Around the edge are five maidenhair ferns (p 99). The arrangement is about 16in high.

Montbretia

Feathers
12 goose sattin feathers, 5in long
27 peacock bracts, as long as possible
Other materials
1 long stem wire
3 short stem wires
binding wire
gutta percha

Centre
Make three bunches of peacock bracts 9in each, and bind each to a short stem wire. Curl them as in Fig 1.
Petals
Trim the fluff from the feathers and cut pointed tips.
Assembly
Arrange four goose sattins, with their slight curve outwards, around each centre and bind tightly. Cover the base of the petals and the stem, Fig 2. Curl the feathers away from the centres. Repeat this for the other two flowers. Assemble a spray of three flowers by joining each stem to the long stem wire, binding with gutta percha, with the binding points about 4in apart. Finally, curve the whole stem slightly.

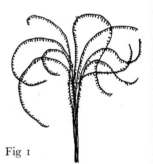

Fig 1

As so many flowers are circular in their form, the montbretia spray provides a welcome change. In arrangements it provides the contrast in shape which is often so badly needed. All the flat flight feathers are suitable for montbretia, but it is advisable to test that the chosen feathers will curl satisfactorily, as this is an important feature of the flower.

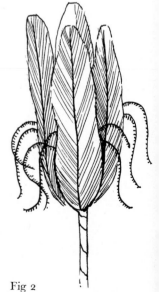

Fig 2

Iris

Feathers
4 goose feathers, 5in long
4 turkey marabout feathers, 4in long
Other materials
1 large pearl bead
12 stem wires
binding wire
gutta percha and glue

Fig 1

Fig 2

Fig 3

Centre
Cover the tip of one of the stem wires with gutta percha, thread on the pearl and cover the remainder, Fig 1.
Petals
Cover eight stem wires with gutta percha and glue one to each of the feathers on the *underside* of the vein, Fig 2. Trim the fluff from the goose feathers, Fig 3.
Assembly
Arrange the four fluffy turkey feathers equally spaced around the centre, allowing them to curve outwards, and bind tightly with wire. Arrange the goose feathers in the spaces between them with the curves inwards. Curve the wires of the fluffy petals in an 'S' shape and curve the upright petals outwards at the base and then inwards, Fig 3. Add three more stem wires to the stem and cover with gutta percha.

The size of these flowers can vary with the feathers used, but the proportions should be such that the 'falls' are wide enough to fill the spaces below the other petals. Irises can be made entirely with non-fluffy feathers, but the sharp curve induced in the 'falls' tends to tear open the barbs of flat feathers, while fluffy ones can better stand the strain. As there are two sorts of petals, there is great scope for colour combinations. Real irises often have 'falls' which are darker than the upright petals. If the upright petals are made darker, the flowers can look top-heavy. These flowers demand space in large arrangements. Their use is restricted by their upright posture, and they appear uncomfortable when placed at an angle.

Crested Lantern

Feathers
6 duck light pearl feathers, 4in long
9 cockerel tails, pieces
Other materials
1 teazel
3 glass beads
1 stem wire
gutta percha and glue

Centre
The teazel forms the centre of the crested lantern and all the petals
are pushed into it. Cut the stem wire into three different lengths. Thread
a bead onto each, securing it with a blob of glue at the end of the wire.
Cover the stems with gutta percha and push them into the top of the
teazel with a little glue, Fig 1.
Petals
The duck feathers are used in their natural state. Cut a pointed piece
3in long from each of the cockerel tails.
Assembly
Push the duck feathers, each with a little glue, curving inwards, into
the teazel about two thirds of the way down the head. The feathers
should almost enclose the beads in the centre. Attach the cockerel tail
pieces, also with a little glue, in a circular arrangement below them,
in a single plane. If the teazel stem is long enough, it needs no covering,
but if it is too short for use in an arrangement, a stem wire should be
added by twisting it round the stem and then covering the whole length
with gutta percha.

With two types of feather in one flower, many variations can be made,
and crest feathers, rather difficult to obtain, make an exciting centre.
The size of the feathers used should be governed by that of the teazel.

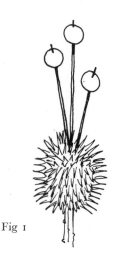

Fig 1

Fig 2

Parrot Tulip

Feathers
5 turkey tail feathers (broads), 6in long
3 goose feathers (biots)
Other materials
6 stem wires
binding wire
gutta percha and glue

ig 1

g 2

g 3

Centre
Curl the biot feathers over a scissor blade so that they form a corkscrew shape without the need for any support. Bunch these together and bind them with binding wire to one of the stem wires, Fig 1.
Petals
These feathers are dyed to contrast with the white biots used for the centre. Cover the five remaining stem wires with *white* gutta percha and glue them along the veins of the turkey feathers on the underside. Shape the feathers so that the petals are pointed, Fig 2. When the glue has dried, curve the wire with the feather the whole way up *against* the natural curve of the feathers. Put a kink in the wire just below the base of the feather to straighten the wire for the stem, Fig 3.
Assembly
Arrange the prepared petals around the central bunch so that they curve inwards, and bind them tightly with binding wire. Finally, cover all the wires and remaining stem with gutta percha.

Make sure that the wire is firmly glued right to the tips of the petals; since the wire is curving the feather against its natural inclinations it will take the slightest opportunity to spring back. A double version of the flower can be made by making twice the number of petals and in the assembly arranging a second circle of petals around the first. Single or double, the flower is quite dramatic in appearance, and is useful for large arrangements.

61

Dewdrop Flower

Feathers
5 body feathers
Other materials
1 glass drop bead
1 stem wire
binding wire
gutta percha

Centre
Cut a short length of binding wire, thread the bead onto it and twist
the end back on itself. Twist this wire end around the stem wire, allowing the bead to stand about an inch proud at the top, Fig 1.

Petals
The small feathers are used in their natural state, with their fluff
retained, Fig 2.

Assembly
Arrange the petals, curved inwards, around the centre and bind tightly
with binding wire. Cover the base of the petals and stem with gutta
percha.

This small flower is really only suitable for the miniature arrangement.

Fig 1

Fig 2

Peony

Feathers
Approximately 9 grey goose cocquilles,
2in long
9 grey goose nagoires, 4in long
Other materials
teazel
glue

Centre
The teazel forms the centre of the peony, and can be dyed if required.
Petals
All the feathers are used in their natural state with all their fluff retained, Fig 1.
Assembly
Each feather is attached by sticking the base first in glue and then into the teazel. First push the cocquilles, curving inwards, into the sides of the teazel approximately half-way up, just allowing the tip of the teazel to remain visible, Fig 2. Push the nagoires into the teazel lower down, also curving inwards, but making a larger cup shape.

The feather peony is for large arrangements. When placed in sunlight, grey goose feathers appear silver. They can be dyed other colours if preferred. The translucent quality of the goose feathers is helpful in making this flower.

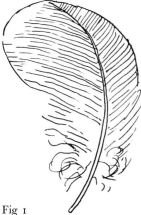

Fig 1

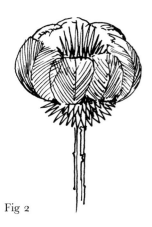

Fig 2

Morning Glory

Feathers
8 golden pheasant green back feathers
Other materials
1 pearl stamen
1 stem wire
binding wire
gutta percha

Centre
The pearl stamen is a ready-made centre, and its stem is simply twisted round the top of the stem wire, Fig 1.

Petals
These golden pheasant back feathers are very dark green with black edges and grey fluff, the colours of which contrast well with the pearl centre. They are used whole in their natural shape, Fig 2.

Assembly
Arrange the petals, curving outwards, around the centre and bind tightly with binding wire. This should kink the central vein of the feather which will allow the petals to open out. Cover the base of the petals and stem with gutta percha. If the feathers do not fan out enough they can be pressed outwards when the flower is assembled; they should form a concave cone.

The fan shape of the feathers is the essential factor in producing this conical shape. Double-bar partridge feathers, turkey cocquilles and golden pheasant collars are some other types which could be used for petals. The simple result is effective when repeated in quantity.

Fig 1

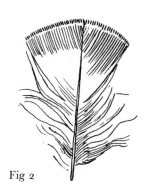

Fig 2

Star Flower Cluster. A block of *Oasis* is wired to the top of a brass kettle stand at the centre of this arrangement, thus raising the flowers from the surface so that they appear to float. The five feathers at the back form a crescent shape for the six star flowers (p 47) to nestle in. The five loop leaves (p 102) are made from four pheasant tail feathers stripped on one side, with the centres filled with wheel tendrils (p 100). Turkey marabout feathers fill the spaces and hide the *Oasis*.

Jacobean Waterlily

Feathers
13 goose nagoires, 6in long
11 goose nagoires, 4in long
Other materials
half an *Oasis* ball
3 stem wires
gutta percha and glue

Centre
Cover all the three stems together with gutta percha. Apply glue to the top and push it into the flat side of the *Oasis*. Curve all the eleven smaller nagoires over a scissor blade, Fig 1. This curls up the whole feather and changes the form of the barbs completely. Push them into the dome of *Oasis* with a little glue, some in the centre with others around them.
Petals
The big feathers are used in their natural state, Fig 2, dyed if required.
Assembly
Push the bigger nagoires, curving inwards, into the centre with a little glue. There should be enough feathers to encircle the centre without overlap.

A large flat arrangement on a plate or tray is probably the best way to display Jacobean waterlilies. With no stems visible, they appear to float, and can look most effective when several, in varying shades, are close together on a tray.

Fig 1

Clematis

Feathers
7 goose nagoires, 6in long
7 cockerel hackles, 4in long
a bunch of ostrich barbs, 3in long
Other materials
binding wire
stem wire
gutta percha and glue

Centre
Dye the ostrich barbs to the required shade. When they are dry tie
them in a bunch with binding wire, Fig 1.
Petals
Dye the goose feathers and the hackles to complete the colour scheme.
As the hackles lie on top of the goose feathers it is attractive to make
them a contrasting colour. Assemble the petals by glueing a hackle
onto the surface of the vein of each goose feather, Fig 2.
Assembly
Arrange the seven petals around the centre with curve outwards and
the hackles on the top surface. Kink the vein of the petals at the junction
with the stem, so they can be bent outwards. Cover the base of the
petals and stem.

Different sizes of feathers can of course be used, and many colour schemes
are possible. This large simple shape is suitable for large arrangements,
but two or three in a small formal design make an elegant low arrangement. The growth habits of the natural clematis can be closely followed
if desired, using a long garland of leaves together with the blooms to
entwine a pillar.

Fig 1

Fig 2

Stem of Stars

Feathers
15 goose feathers, 4in long
Other materials
15 wooden beads
2 stem wires
binding wire
gutta percha

Centre

Divide the beads into three groups of five. Thread a piece of binding wire through each bead; bend the wire over and twist it to secure the bead, leaving a stem of 2 or 3in. Then twist each group together to make three bunches, Fig 1. Cut one of the two stem wires in half, then bind each bunch of beads with binding wire to the top of a stem. There will thus be one long stem and two short ones.

Petals

The goose feathers are used with any fluff removed, and the tips cut to a point, Fig 2.

Assembly

Arrange four petals, curving outwards, around one of the bunches of beads and bind them on with binding wire, allowing the beads to protrude from the centre. Repeat this with the two other bunches. Take the long flower and bind the base of the petals and *one third* of the stem with gutta percha; repeat this with the other two, covering the whole of their stems. Join the second flower to the long stem at the point where the binding stopped and bind the two together with gutta percha. When the third flower is added in the same way, the flowers should be equally spaced down the stem, and the whole stem covered with binding.

Contour feathers with as little fluff as possible are best for stems of stars. These can be dyed, as can the beads, to make coloured stars. These flowers are useful in an arrangement as they contrast well with circular flowers.

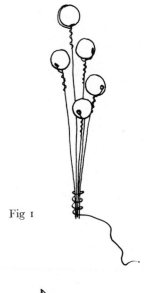

Fig 1

Fig 2

Bead Daisy

Feathers
8 ostrich body feathers, 4in long
Other materials
approximately 36 small glass beads
short pins
Styrofoam ball
stem wire
gutta percha and glue

Centre
Cover the stem wire with gutta percha, apply glue to the top and push
it into the *Styrofoam* ball. Thread each bead onto a pin and push it into
the ball until the top half of the ball is covered with beads, Fig 1.
Petals
Trim each feather to a pointed oval shape, Fig 2.
Assembly
Push the petals into the *Styrofoam* ball with a little glue so that they lie
absolutely flat in a single plane.

The ostrich body feathers are particularly suitable because they are
not only flat but also have a clearly defined centre vein which helps
the appearance of the finished flower. These feathers can be bought
already dyed in many colours. Beads, too, come in many colours and
so there is plenty of opportunity for variation.

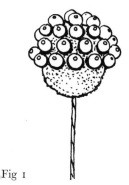

Fig 1

Fig 2

69

Pearly Flower Bud

Feathers
5 goose nagoires, 5in long
Other materials
1 pearl bead
1 stem wire
binding wire
gutta percha and glue

Centre
Dip the end of the stem wire in glue and thread on the bead. Cover the rest of the stem with gutta percha, Fig 1.
Petals
Trim the fluff from the base of the feathers, Fig 2.
Assembly
Place a petal, curving inwards, on each side of the centre, covering the bead, and bind tightly. Add the remaining petals in the gaps left by the first two. Cover the base of the petals and the stem with gutta percha.

Fig 1

Pearly flowers will be particularly useful for arrangements requiring large flowers, and the bud gives variety. Goose feathers make the best pearly flowers. Should a different flower size be required, make sure that the same balance is kept between the centre and petal size. Small pearly flowers can be made with smaller feathers, but larger feathers are too narrow to make petals for this flower, and of course adding to the number of petals alters the design.

Fig 2

Pearly Flower

Feathers
8 goose nagoires, 6in long
Other materials
12 pearl beads
13 or more stem wires
binding wire
gutta percha and glue

Centre
Dip the ends of twelve of the stem wires in glue and thread a bead on each. Cover the rest of each stem with gutta percha. Make a bunch of them, varying their heights, and bind them with wire approximately half-way down their length. Add the remaining stem wire to this point. If the single stem wire will not support this rather heavy centre, additional wires can be added to keep the centre erect, Fig 1.

Petals
Trim the fluff from the feathers and kink the vein of each one 5in from the top, Fig 2.

Assembly
Arrange the petals, curving outwards, around the centre and bind them tightly to the main stem where the feathers were kinked. Cover the base of the petals and stem with gutta percha. Ease the petals out slightly away from the centre.

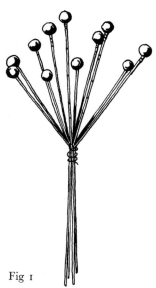

Fig 1

Fig 2

French Partridge Flower

Feathers
7 red partridge feathers
Other materials
6 glass beads
small piece of *Oasis*
1 stem wire
binding wire
gutta percha and glue

Centre
Cut a small piece of *Oasis* about 1in across and fix it to the top of the stem wire with glue. Cover the stem with gutta percha. Cut six short lengths of binding wire and thread a bead on to each, securing it by twisting the wire back on itself, Fig 1. Push the bead stems into the *Oasis* with a little glue, Fig 2.

Petals
The partridge feathers are used in their natural state, with their fluff retained.

Assembly
Push the feathers, curving outwards, into the *Oasis* with a little glue, so that they encircle the beads.

This can be tricky if the *Oasis* is old and crumbly, or if the piece is too small, as the whole flower disintegrates all too easily. It is, however, a good way to display the subtle colouring of the French partridge feathers. Interesting experiments can be tried using other small patterned feathers. These small flowers are surprisingly effective from a distance.

ig 1

ig 2

Silver Primrose. Helter skelter tendrils (p 96) are the only leaves which accompany the silver primroses (p 76). This arrangement is especially suitable for the dining table lit with candles.

Miniature Arrangement. Seven cherry flowers (p 43) are arranged informally with several couch grasses (p 94). Below the flowers are disc leaves interspersed with dried rushes. The whole arrangement is about 6in high.

Sunburst

Feathers
35 ostrich body feathers, 3in long
Other materials
21 small beads
4 stem wires
gutta percha and glue

Centre
Cut four of the stem wires in half. Take seven of the eight short pieces and thread three small beads on each. Secure the top with glue and cover the remainder of the stem with gutta percha, Fig 1.

Petals
Trim all the ostrich feathers to a pointed oval shape and pull off any surplus fluff at the back, Fig 2.

Assembly
The sunburst consists of seven small flowers wired together to form one large bloom. To make each of the seven, arrange five feather petals curving outwards around the beaded stem and secure tightly with binding wire. Cover the base of the petals and cover the stem for the second time, Fig 3. When all seven flowers are assembled, bunch them together at the base and bind the whole lot tightly with binding wire. Separate the little flowers until the head is dome-shaped. Then cover the base of the bunch and the stem.

Many of the larger flowers have a single, rather solid, shape. The multiflower head of the sunburst makes just as large a bloom, but as the light passes through it, the effect is not so heavy. Because the small individual flowers are made from small feathers, there are many possible substitutes. As the general outline and appearance of the sunburst is not particularly sharp, a simple but dramatic flower should be chosen to accompany it in a design.

Fig 1

Fig 2

Fig 3

Frosted Pine Lily

Feathers
12 crest feathers, varying lengths
8 goose cocquilles, 3in long
Other materials
1 *Styrofoam* ball
3 stem wires
gutta percha and glue

Centre
Cover the three stem wires together with gutta percha. Apply glue to the top and push it into the *Styrofoam* ball. Using the longest crest feathers, push them into the top of the ball with a little glue. Put the remaining feathers into the top, allowing each one to stand free, Fig 1.

Petals
The cocquilles are used in their natural state, Fig 2, but dyed if required.

Assembly
Push the cocquilles into the *Styrofoam* ball with a little glue around its 'equator'. Arrange them not only curved outwards but backwards as well, to give emphasis to the crest feathers extending out of the centre. Bend the stem over so that the flower head points downwards. The petals should hide the rear of the ball, but some tiny feathers can be glued to its surface at the back if desired.

This flower design is useful for displaying any exceptional or rare feathers.

ig 1

ig 2

Silver Primrose

Feathers
6 pigeon body feathers, 2in long
Other materials
1 wooden bead
foil acetate
5 stem wires
binding wire
gutta percha and glue

Centre
Cut a small piece of binding wire, thread it through the bead, and twist
both ends together to secure the bead in the centre, Fig 1.
Petals
Cover all the stem wires with gutta percha. Cut six shapes $2\frac{1}{2}$in long
from the acetate, pointed at the base and rounded at the tip. The size is
governed by the feathers used—the mount should be a little larger all
round than the feather. Glue a stem wire up the centre of the mount to
within an inch of the top. The wire is now on the top surface of the
mount, Fig 2. Apply glue to the surface of the wire and place a feather
with its tip curving away from the mount, Fig 3. Repeat this with each
of the other feathers. Bend all the stem wires backwards at right angles
at the base of the petals.
Assembly
Arrange the petals around the centre and bind them together tightly,
covering the whole stem with gutta percha.

The foil acetate used for these silver primroses makes them particularly
suitable for the dining table, especially when they reflect the light of
candles. The use of acetate, whether silver or coloured, gives a definite
outline to the petals, and care is necessary when combining them with
others in an arrangement, as they are modern shapes. The flatness of
the flower form can be offset if some of the stems are bent at right angles
just below the head.

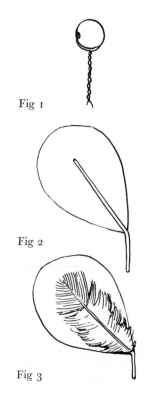

Fig 1

Fig 2

Fig 3

76

Begonia

Feathers
18 turkey tail feathers—'broads'
6in or more long
Other materials
6 beads
21 stem wires
binding wire
gutta percha and glue

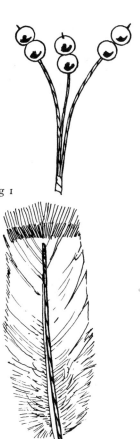

ig 1

g 2

Centre
Thread two beads on each of three stem wires. Secure with glue at the top and cover the remaining part of each wire with gutta percha. Bind them together in a bunch and curve their stems outwards slightly, Fig 1.
Petals
Cut six of the turkey feathers to 4in in length, and the remaining twelve to 6in, cutting from the bottom and retaining the tip. Cover the remaining stem wires with gutta percha and glue one to the back of the centre vein of each of the feathers, Fig 2. Allow all the feathers to keep their natural curve by curving the stem wires to match.
Assembly
Arrange the six smaller petals around the centre and bind tightly. Arrange six of the larger ones in the spaces and bind tightly before adding the six remaining petals. Cover the base of the petals and the stem with gutta percha.

These flowers will be too large for many of the more conventional arrangements. They can, however, look very well if arranged on their own, as do sunflowers. Their striking shape and form make them clearly defined from a distance. If a longer stem is required, several stem wires will be needed together to support the very heavy weight of the flower head. Turkey feathers have a particularly broad, flat shape, well maintained right to the tip. If you can find another feather with the same shape, it will do just as well.

Cactus Flower

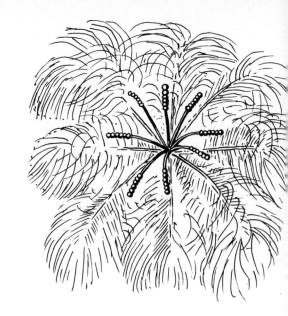

Feathers
8 turkey marabout feathers, 6in long
Other materials
48 silver beads
16 or more stem wires
binding wire
gutta percha and glue

Centre
Thread six beads onto each of eight stem wires and cover the remainder of the stem in each case with gutta percha. Make a bunch of these and bind tightly together one third of the way down, curving each stem out slightly, Fig 1.

Petals
Cover the remaining eight stem wires with gutta percha and glue one to the underside of the vein of each marabout feather, Fig 2. Curve the wire to follow the natural curve of the feather.

Assembly
Arrange the feathers, curving outwards, around the centre and bind tightly with binding wire below the base of the petals. Cover the whole stem. Bend each petal outwards at its base so that the centre beads stand clearly away from the petals.

As this is a very large exotic flower, its use is limited to large arrangements, or those in which it is the centrepiece. The marabout feathers are most suitable because they are so fluffy. If down feathers—equally fluffy—are used, the other constituents of the flower have to be scaled down in size to match. A slight draught will keep this flower quivering attractively.

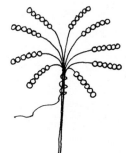

Fig 1

Fig 2

Hollyhocks and Carnations. As both hollyhocks (p 41) and carnations (p 86) are made with golden pheasant collar feathers they happily combine in the same vase.

Protea

Feathers
approximately 36 pheasant back
feather tips
22 pigeon wing feathers
Other materials
half an *Oasis* ball
3 stem wires
gutta percha and glue

Centre
Cover the three stem wires, all together, with gutta percha, apply glue
to the top and push it into the flat part of the *Oasis*. Cut the tips from
all the pheasant feathers and push them into the *Oasis* dome, with a
little glue, placing them so that they stand up all over the surface of the
Oasis, Fig 1.
Petals
Cut diagonally across the top of all the pigeon feathers, leaving them
2in long, and ignoring the structure of the feather, Fig 2. These feathers
can be dyed to blend with those used for the centre.
Assembly
Push the pigeon feathers into the *Oasis* with a little glue all round the
very edge, taking care that the angle at which these feathers are placed
causes them to enclose the centre.

This flower is inspired by the unusual South African flowers of the
same name. In choosing substitute feathers, a strong contrast in types
of feather should be sought. This rather stiff flower is an excellent foil
for an arrangement of fragile light flowers.

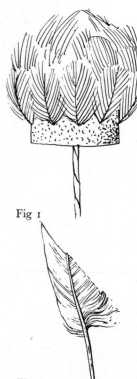

Fig 1

Fig 2

Peacock Flower

Feathers
5 peacock tails (eyes only used)
many pheasant body feathers
Other materials
5 pearl beads
cartridge paper
binding wire
10 stem wires
gutta percha and glue

Centre
Apply glue to five of the stem wires and attach one bead onto the top of each. Cover the remainder of these stems with gutta percha. Arrange them in a bunch, all the same length, and bind them with binding wire 1in from the top, Fig 1.

ig 1

Petals
These are mounted petals, so first cut five simple pointed petal shapes from the paper, Fig 2. As a rough guide, the paper mount should be the same shape as the peacock eye, though larger. Trim the whiskers and carefully cut the eyes from five peacock tail feathers. Draw a line of glue up the centre of each petal shape and stick on a stem wire. This forms the top surface of the petal onto which the feathers are mounted. Apply a layer of glue about 1in wide around the edge of one of the petals. Attach the pheasant feathers, radiating from the base of the petal and overlapping the edge of the mount, Fig 3. Now put glue on the centre area and stick the peacock eye into this space. Repeat this with the other four petals. Bend all the stems back at the base of the petals.

ig 2

Assembly
Arrange the petals around the centre and bind the whole bunch of stems with gutta percha.

It takes a bit of courage to cut out the best part of a beautiful peacock tail feather, but it is the eye which is the making of this flower. Whilst being suitable for large arrangements, mounted peacock flowers can make a composition on their own.

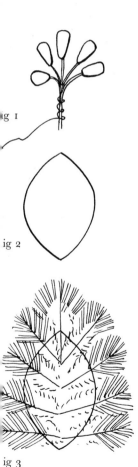

ig 3

Tropical Lily

Feathers
14 church windows, tips
approximately 22 cockerel hackles, 6in long
12 pigeon body feathers, 2in long
6 cockerel tail, tips
3 pheasant red spears, various lengths
8 pheasant back, tips

Other materials
half a ball of *Oasis*
3 stem wires
gutta percha and glue

Centre
The *Oasis* forms the centre, although when the flower is completed this is not seen. Push the three stem wires into the flat part of the half ball of *Oasis*, a little apart, binding them together.

Petals
The cockerel hackles and pigeon feathers are used in their whole state. Cut the tips from the church windows, pheasant back and cockerel tails—six pieces cut from one cockerel tail will do, if insufficient feathers are available. Strip the fluff from the red spears.

Assembly
Push the hackles into the *Oasis* all round the edge so that they just touch each other. Care should be taken here to ensure that all the feathers lie in a single arc. Then push the church window tips into the *Oasis*, arranging them to lie on the surface of the hackles in a second, smaller ring, Fig 1. Apply glue to the rest of the ball and lay the cockerel tail tips flat on the surface, making their points touch at the centre, Fig 2. Next make a ring of pigeon body feathers and insert these in a rosette between the church windows and the cockerel tail tips, Fig 3. Finally add the three red spears to the centre of the dome. The tips of the pheasant back feathers can be glued to the uncovered *Oasis* at the back if required. Cover the stem with gutta percha and bend the whole flower head over at more than a right angle, so that the flower points diagonally downwards.

This is a very exotic flower, and it can look uncomfortable and over-dressed when associated with other, simpler flowers. A single flower can be displayed on its own, and many other combinations of feathers can be tried.

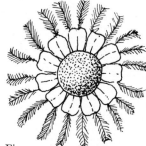

Fig 1

Fig 2

Fig 3

Sun Lily

Feathers
9 goose nagoires, 8in long
9 goose cocquilles, 9in long
9 goose cocquilles, 4in long
9 goose biots
Other materials
half an *Oasis* ball
4 stem wires
gutta percha

Centre
Dye the biots if required to make a suitable colour for the centre. Make three bunches each of three biots, and bind them separately with short pieces cut from one of the stem wires. Cover the wires with gutta percha. Curve each one separately over a scissor blade so that they all curl in different directions, as shown in Fig 1.

Petals
Dye the nagoires if required. The cocquilles are all used in their natural state, their fluff is left on and their natural curve retained, but they, too, can be dyed if required. Shave off the back of the vein of the nagoires with a blade, and then curve the vein over a scissor blade, taking care not to curl up the contour part, Fig 2.

Assembly
Push the three stem wires into the back of the *Oasis*, slightly apart, and bind them together with gutta percha. Push the curly feathers into the *Oasis* all round the edge, allowing them to curl right back to the stem, Fig 3. Using the largest cocquilles, push them into the *Oasis* near to the nagoires, allowing them to lie on the surface, and next push all the small cocquilles into the centre, curving outwards; these feathers should fill the remaining space. Finally, add the three bunches of biots by pushing them right into the middle, curving their stems over together so that they appear to tumble out of the sun lily as a cascade.

A giant flower, this is really more suitable for the Japanese type of arrangement (where a very few blooms are used to create line and shape) than one of conventional style. There is plenty of opportunity for varying the colour scheme by dyeing, but plain feathers are better than patterned ones. Goose feathers have exactly the right quality for this billowing bloom.

Fig 1

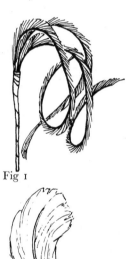

Fig 2

Fig 3

Arrow Flower

Feathers
7 goose nagoires, 6in long
Other materials
Styrofoam ball
19 large glass beads
19 pins
3 stem wires
gutta percha and glue

Fig 1

Centre
Cover the three stem wires all together with gutta percha, apply glue to the top of the resulting stalk and push it into the *Styrofoam* ball. Thread each bead onto a pin and push the pins into the ball with a little glue, Fig 1. Ensure that the beads touch one another and that they cover three-quarters of the ball.
Petals
Dye the feathers to match or contrast with the colour of the beads. They are to be used in their natural shape, Fig 2.
Assembly
Push the feathers, with a little glue, into the ball, in the space between the beads and the stem, so that they curve backwards.

This flower should be displayed pointing downwards; the heaviness of the beads will weigh it down anyway. Its striking shape contrasts well with more conventional flowers. For Christmas decorations, gold or silver beads can be substituted for the glass ones.

Fig 2

Florentine Panel. A cardboard panel was drawn up with crossing diagonal lines in pencil, spaced at regular intervals. Starting at the top, a row of matching feathers was glued in close sequence along the zigzag produced by the diagonals. Layer upon layer was added until the panel was completely covered. All the feathers in this panel come from a ring-necked pheasant, ensuring uniformity in the colour scheme.

Carnation

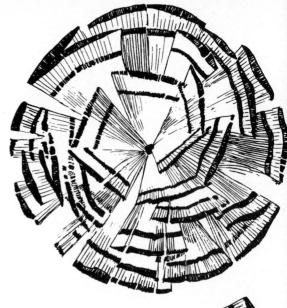

Feathers
approximately 27 golden pheasant
collar feathers
Other materials
1 stem wire
binding wire
gutta percha

Centre
The flower does not need a centre, though a simple bead can be used
if preferred.

Petals
Each feather should be curved over a scissor blade near its base, Fig 1.

Fig 1

Assembly
Make a bunch of three feathers and bind them tightly to the top of
the stem wire, Fig 2. Then add the rest of the petals individually at
regular intervals around the stem until all are used up. Cover the base
of the petals and the stem with gutta percha. If the petals do not make
an attractive fan, they can be persuaded to do so by pressing them by
hand once the flower is assembled.

Double-bar partridge feathers can be substituted, giving a stripe along
the top of each petal. This is an extremely adaptable flower and is
invaluable in mixed arrangements.

Fig 2

Fuchsia

Feathers
6 goose cocquilles, 3in long
7 French partridge feathers, 2in long
Other materials
3 glass drop beads
1 stem wire
binding wire
gutta percha

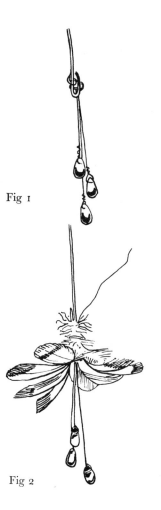

Fig 1

Fig 2

Centre
Cut three pieces of binding wire and attach a bead to each by twisting the stem back on itself, Fig 1. Arrange these into a bunch and attach them to the stem wire by binding with binding wire.
Petals
Both types of feather are used in their natural state, retaining the fluff. Should they require dyeing, make sure they are restored to their original shape before they are used for fuchsias. Sometimes a complementary colour scheme can be achieved by dyeing only one of the feather types.
Assembly
Arrange the partridge feathers, curving outwards, around the bunch of beads and bind tightly with stem wire, Fig 2. Arrange the goose cocquilles around the rest with the curve outwards and also bind tightly with binding wire. If the veins of the cocquilles have been kinked, they can be pushed slightly away from the partridge feather 'skirt'. Finally, cover the base of the petals and stem with gutta percha and hook the whole stem over so that the fuchsia hangs down.

The characteristics of fuchsias are easily recognisable, and, provided the whole flower hangs down and the petals curl outwards to reveal beads falling out of the centre, the actual choice of feathers is limitless. Because of their pendulous habit, fuchsias in an arrangement should be allowed to cascade over the edge of the vase. In this way they will fill the awkward gap between the arrangement and the surface on which it stands.

Fuchsias can be made with many different feathers, and the essential strong curve is present in most of the small feathers. Beautiful contrasts can be achieved with one flower by using the golden pheasant's orange collar feathers with plain white ones. Jungle-cock breast feathers also make delicate fuchsias.

5 *Making the Leaves*

Simple Leaf

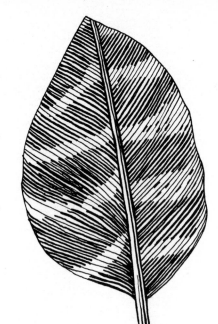

Feathers

1 turkey wing feather

Leaf

Leaving about 4in of the tip of the feather, strip off all the rest of the bracts and fluff. Trim the top to a pointed shape.

This basic leaf is the simplest one to make and is surprisingly realistic. The stripped vein makes the stem and it always has a natural curve in sympathy with the leaf.

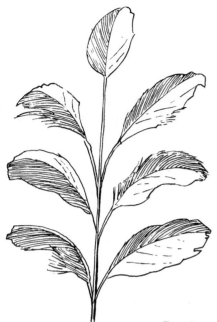

Bi-coloured Leaves

Feathers
7 goose nagoires, 5in long
Other materials
4 stem wires
binding wire
gutta percha

Leaf
These leaves are variegated because the feathers are dyed or painted on one side only of their width. The vein usefully prevents the paint from straying onto the other side. Trim off the fluff, Fig 1.

Assembly
Cut three of the stem wires in half to make six short stems and one long one. Join a feather to the top of each stem with binding wire. Cover all the stems and bases of the feathers with gutta percha, leaving half of the long stem uncovered. At a point 5in down the long stem join a pair of leaves, one on either side, allowing the leaves to have a stem of about 2in in length. Cover the main stem for 5in more, then add another two leaves as before. Repeat with the final pair. Bend all the leaves away from the main stem.

These leaves are simple in form and surprisingly realistic in appearance. They are useful in all kinds of arrangements, and for further variations both sides of the leaves can be painted, or spray paints can be used.

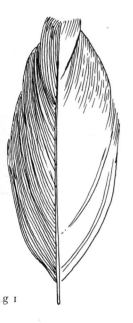

g 1

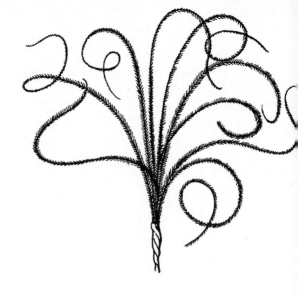

Feather Grass

Feathers
9 bracts of peacock tails
Other materials
stem wire
binding wire
gutta percha

Assembly
Curl the bracts over a scissor blade, Fig 1. Bunch them together and join to the top of the stem wire by binding with binding wire, Fig 2. Cover the base of the feathers and stem.

It is easy to see how the plant feather grass received its name, and it is quite hard to tell the difference between the real and the artificial in an arrangement. The wispy appearance of the grass contrasts well with flowers like the pearly flower and the daisies.

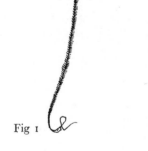

Fig 1

Fig 2

Willow

Feathers
7 goose pilets, as long as possible
Other materials
long stem wire
binding wire
gutta percha

Leaf
Choose the pilets so that three come from one side of the bird and four from the other side, Fig 1.
Assembly
Choose the straightest feather and bind it to the top of the stem wire. Continue binding for 2 in down the wire. Join two feathers at this point, curving outwards on either side, and bind tightly with binding wire so as to kink the veins. Continue binding the stem for another 2in and join a further pair of feathers. Repeat for the last pair and cover the remaining stem.

The leaves of the willow can also be made with cockerel hackles, which are similar in size and shape to the pilets. Like many leaves, these willows add to the shape of an arrangement, without adding much weight.

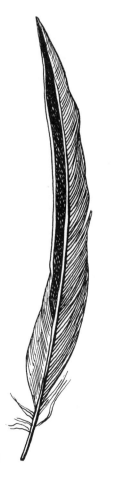

Fig 1

Traveller's Joy

Feathers
18 cockerel hackles
Other materials
long stem wires
binding wire
gutta percha

Leaf
Dye the hackles if required. When they are dry, curl them to a spiral form over a scissor blade.

Assembly
Make six bunches each of three feathers and bind each bunch tightly with binding wire, Fig 1. Join one to the top of the stem wire, covering the base of the feathers and about 4in of the stem with gutta percha. Add a second bunch in the same manner, and then continue with the rest at 4in intervals down the stem. Finally, shape the whole stem into a spiral, starting at the top and working downwards.

A useful addition to a 'solid' arrangement. When flowers are arranged in a vase on a stand or in a candlestick, the traveller's joy can be made to twist round the stem.

Fig 1

Floating Discs. These discs vary in their appearance according to the feathers which are used. A piece of shiny black card with a wet appearance makes them seem to float.

92

Couch Grass

Feathers
15 teal breast feathers
Other materials
1 stem wire
binding wire
gutta percha

Assembly
Cover the stem wire with gutta percha. Divide the feathers into three equal groups. Arrange the five feathers from one group, curving outwards, around the top of the stem wire and bind tightly with binding wire, Fig 1. Repeat with the two remaining groups, placing them successively lower down the stem at intervals of about 1in. These feathers are so tiny that the binding wire is hardly seen and therefore need not be covered with gutta percha.

This grass is useful for miniature arrangements. Any strongly curved breast feather will create the right shape for couch grass, but naturally the size of the feather will govern the final size of the grass. It may be necessary to add more feathers to each group to ensure that each 'ring' is without gaps. The feathers used here are really forming the seed heads of the grass, and this may be made with more than three 'rings' if preferred.

Fig 1

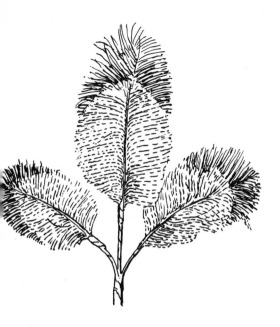

Layered Leaf

Feathers
6 ostrich body feathers, varying sizes
Other materials
2 stem wires
binding wire
gutta percha and glue

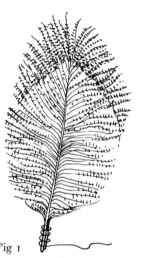

Leaf
Take out the three largest feathers and dye these to contrast in colour with the smaller ones.
Assembly
Cut one of the stem wires in half to make a total of three stems, one long and two short. Arrange the feathers in pairs, each pair consisting of a large dyed feather and a small undyed one. Glue the pairs of feathers together, sandwiching a stem wire in each, Fig 1. Join all the three stems together, the large one in the centre, and cover them with gutta percha. Bend the stems so that the three parts of the leaf are touching, as in the finished drawing.

This fluffy leaf is a good contrast to some of the simpler flower shapes. Because of the two colours used, the leaf appears to have a halo. The small feathers can be dyed and the large ones left plain if preferred.

Fig 1

Helter Skelter Tendril

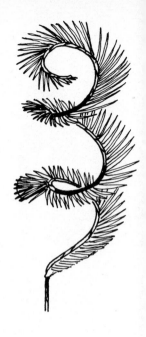

Feathers
1 biot feather, as long as possible
Other materials
1 stem wire
gutta percha and glue

Assembly
Cover the stem wire with gutta percha. Apply glue to the flat surface
of the biot feather. Stick this to the stem wire, Fig 1, holding the top
until the glue is dry. Then hold the top of the wire half-way up the index
finger with the thumb, and bind the wire, with the biot on the outside,
around the finger, using the other hand. When the top of the index finger is reached, and the pressure at both ends of the spiral is eased, it
can be taken off the finger carefully, retaining its spiral form. The
remainder of the stem can be bent if required.

Biots are the only feathers which will fan out in this way to accentuate
a spiral. Care should be taken during the glueing to ensure that no
glue prevents the barbs separating. While this tendril is useful in small
arrangements, it can also make an exotic centre to a large flower. If a
second biot is used and spiralled in the same way, the two can be joined
together to make a double helix, Fig 2.

Fig 1

Fig 2

Bulrush

Feathers
many teal breast feathers
Other materials
Oasis
long stem wire
gutta percha and glue

Assembly
Cut a cylinder from the *Oasis* using, if you have one, an apple corer. You will need a cylinder about 8in long, or alternatively two shorter ones joined end to end. Thread them onto the stem wire, allowing them to touch. Cover the remainder of the stem with gutta percha, Fig 1. Starting at the top, push in the small teal feathers one by one, curved inwards, until the *Oasis* is completely hidden.

The size of these bulrush heads is determined by the diameter and length of the *Oasis* cylinder. If no apple corer is available, the *Oasis* can of course be cut to the required shape with a knife. The basis for a giant bulrush can be made by using a plain pastry cutter to cut the cylinders. Any small body feathers can be used, provided they have a strong natural curve.

Fig 1

Maidenhair Fern

Feathers
5 pheasant gold sides, varying lengths
Other materials
1 stem wire
binding wire
gutta percha

Leaf
Choose the five feathers from opposite sides of the bird, so that when held in a fan those on each side are mirror images of one another with the remaining out in the centre. Strip off the fluff, and then the barbs from the sides of the feathers, leaving only 1 in of the feather on the top, Fig 1.

Assembly
Arrange the feathers in a fan shape around the stem wire. Bind tightly with binding wire. The pressure on the veins of the feathers will cause them to fan out. Cover the ends of the feathers and the stem wire with gutta percha. Curve the stem very slightly in profile to make it a gentle 'S' shape.

Alternative feathers can be used for this fern. Patterned feathers can give fronds detailed interest if desired. Larger maidenhair ferns can be made by arranging these single branches in fans. In doing this, always cover each branch completely with gutta percha before joining the next, otherwise the joint will twist.

Fig 1

Design in a Dolphin Vase. This dolphin vase is a popular and convenient shape for displaying feather flowers. Two roses (p 36), made with pheasant red hearts, and four French partridge flowers (p 75) form the centre cluster. The background consists of plain macaw feathers, contrasting with four curly leaf sprays (p 104).

Wheel Tendril

Feathers
1 biot feather, as long as possible
Other materials
1 stem wire
gutta percha and glue

Assembly
This wheel tendril, Fig 1, is similar to the helter skelter tendril, the only difference being the direction in which the wire is curved. Starting at the tip, attach the biot to the stem wire as with the helter skelter tendril, and make a tight curl in a single plane, and straighten out the rest of the stem.

This tendril is effective on its own, and can also be used as a centre for loop leaves. The flat form of the wheel tendril makes it useful for flower pictures too. The length of the biot feather controls the size of the spiral. It is difficult to join two biots without showing an ugly join.

Fig 1

Variegated Ivy Leaf

Feathers
10 ostrich body feathers, 5 large, 5 small
Other materials
cartridge paper
stem wire
binding wire
gutta percha and glue

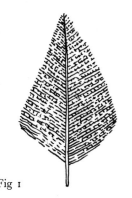

Fig 1

Leaf
Dye five of the feathers, either the large or the small ones, so that they contrast with the undyed ones. Trim all the feathers to a simple pointed shape, Fig 1.

Assembly
Cut the piece of paper to an ivy-leaf shape approximately 3in long by 3in wide, Fig 2. Cover the stem wire with gutta percha and glue it to the centre of the paper leaf. Apply glue to the largest of the large feathers and place it on the paper leaf pointing towards the tip. Repeat the process with the other four feathers, directing them towards the other points. Apply glue to the remaining five feathers and place them on the large ones so that a rim of contrasting colour can be seen around the edge. The paper mount will be completely hidden.

A covered stem of any length can be made and the leaves attached at intervals alternately on either side. Ostrich body feathers are particularly suitable owing to their breadth and comparative firmness. If the backs of the leaves show, the paper mount must be covered by attaching feathers to this side too.

Fig 2

Loop Leaf

Feathers
3 goose pilets, as long as possible
Other materials
Stem wire
binding wire
gutta percha

Leaf
Each feather makes one looped leaf. Join each tip to its own base and secure with binding wire, Fig 1.
Assembly
Attach one leaf to the top of the stem wire with gutta percha and continue the binding down for 2in. Join the next at this point and cover the stem for a further 2in. Then attach the third loop and cover the remainder of the stem.

Only very long, thin and flexible feathers can be used for loop leaves. Hackles and pheasant tail feathers can be successfully used. The pheasant feathers are larger than the pilets and may well be more satisfactory if used singly on a stem. The hole in the loop can be filled with a wheel tendril if desired.

Fig 1

Seed Head

Feathers
6 biots, as long as possible
Other materials
large wooden bead
7 stem wires
binding wire
gutta percha and glue

Seed head
Cover six of the stem wires with gutta percha and glue one biot to each one, Fig 1.
Assembly
Hold all the tips together in a bunch, with the stalks pointing upwards, and bind the tips tightly with binding wire. Apply glue to this binding and thread on the bead, Fig 2. Bend all the stems right out, round and down until they meet together in a bunch below the bead. Bind them with binding wire and cover with gutta percha, adding the remaining stem wire to make the stem.

This is an unusual design, more particularly suitable for modern arrangements. If the seed heads are allowed to stand free of any flowers, light will pass through and clearly show the bead in the centre. The biot feathers can be dyed if desired.

Fig 1

Fig 2

Curly Leaves

Feathers
9 ostrich body feathers
Other materials
1 long stem wire
binding wire
gutta percha

Leaf
Steam all the feathers to make them as fluffy as possible. Curl each one over a scissor blade, Fig 1.
Assembly
Join one feather to the top of the stem wire by binding with binding wire. Cover the joint and about 2in of the stem with gutta percha. Join the remaining feathers in a similar manner down the stem on alternate sides. Finally, curve the whole stem very gently in one direction.

These curved stems can be used to produce flowing lines in otherwise stiff arrangements. The texture contrasts well if used in a composition with single large feathers like pheasant tail feathers.

Fig 1

Tulips, Palms and Roses. These flowers are arranged in a pedestal vase filled with *Oasis*. Three parrot tulips (p 61) run through the centre of the design. Double-bar partridge feathers are used for the roses. The feathery outlines of the palms (p 106) enlarge and soften the whole composition. Stems of stars complete it.

Biot Palm

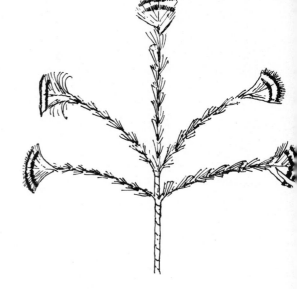

Feathers
5 biot feathers, 9in or as long as possible
5 partridge feathers, tips
Other materials
6 stem wires
gutta percha and glue

Leaf
Cover five of the stem wires with gutta percha. Apply glue along the whole length of the flat side on one of the biots. Starting at the top of one of the stem wires, attach the tip of the biot and, holding it firmly, slowly rotate the stem, allowing the biot to stick as it spirals downward, Fig 1. Cut the partridge tips about 1in long and glue one to the top of the biot spiral, Fig 2. Repeat this with the other four stems.

Assembly
Cover the sixth stem wire with gutta percha. The five feathered stems should be arranged in a fan shape, and attached *one after the other* to the sixth or master stem. Using the largest one first, attach it so that it forms a continuation of the master stem. The others should then be added one at a time, but placed in pairs, on either side. Cover the lower part of the stem again with gutta percha. Further stem wires can be added here for support if necessary. Curve the side fronds away from the central one to form a fan shape. Make sure, when applying glue to the biots, that no glue touches the barbs, or they will not separate to form an even spiral. When assembling the fan, take care that the fronds of the partridge tips face forwards.

This is a difficult leaf to make, but the effort is well worth making. The biot palm is useful in large designs.

Fig 1

Fig 2

Disc Leaf

Feathers
1 cockerel tail tip
7 golden pheasant gold back tips
Other materials
cartridge paper
2 stem wires
gutta percha and glue

Leaf

Cut one paper mount 2in long in the shape indicated in Fig 1, and glue a stem wire up its centre. Use the tips from all the gold back feathers.

Assembly

Cover the whole surface of the mount with glue and arrange the gold tips around the edge so that they overlap the edge, Fig 2. Fill the centre with a cockerel tail tip, then curve the whole leaf gently into a convex shape.

The intricate detail on this leaf can provide an interesting contrast to plain-petalled flowers. These small leaves can be arranged in sprays if desired.

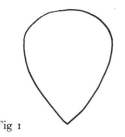

Fig 1

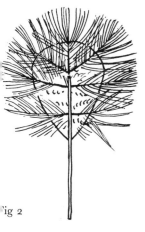

Fig 2

Mimosa Leaf

Feathers
13 cockerel hackles, 5in long
1 biot
Other materials
acetate film
1 stem wire
gutta percha and glue

Fig 1

Leaf
Cut a simple pointed leaf shape from the acetate film, Fig 1. Cover the stem wire with gutta percha and glue it on the surface of the acetate leaf mount from tip to base. One must be patient in sticking gutta percha to acetate, and avoid moving the leaf until it is quite dry. The wire is on the upper surface of the leaf mount.

Assembly
Glue one of the hackles on top of the wire, allowing it to overlap the mount, Fig 2. Glue the remaining hackles, six on each side, on the face of the mount. They should lie diagonally to the central 'vein' with their bases pointing downwards to touch the wire in the centre. Make sure all the feathers overlap the edge of the mount. Next glue the biot up the centre vein on its edge to produce a three-dimensional effect. When all the glue is dry, the whole leaf can be curved.

The natural white colour of the hackles is effective when placed on a coloured mount, their thin nature allowing the colour to show through. Use mimosa leaves horizontally for the best effect. They look well in table centres when combined with crisp simple flowers.

Fig 2

Arrangement with Goose Feathers. Every flower in this arrangement has petals of goose feathers. A snowball (p 50) is surrounded by six peonies (p 63) and several crested pigeon lilies (p 56). Around the edge are peacock feathers, the barbs of which are used for the centres of the lilies (see top right). There are three more lilies in the front with cat's-tail grasses as their centres. They all stand in a dark blue vase which is an effective foil to the silvery grey feathers of the goose.

Bracken

Feathers
19 chicken body feathers, 3in long
Other materials
6 long stem wires
gutta percha and glue

Leaf
Choose the chicken feathers for uniformity, and arrange them in pairs.
Assembly
Make two long stem wires by binding the stem wires together in threes, with the three wires side by side so that the resulting bound stem is flat in section. Put dots of glue 1 in apart on one side of one of the flat stems. Place the shafts of the feathers on the glue in pairs with their bases overlapping, Fig 1. When all the feathers have been attached, put more glue onto the point where the shafts cross, and press on the other wire stem, sandwiching all the feathers between the two stems. When the glue is dry, gently curve the stem to an 'S'-shaped curve.

Just like real bracken, feather bracken can be used to enlarge arrangements. Chicken feathers are effective because of the contrast between their light fluff and brown tips, but other body feathers can be used equally well.

Fig 1

Star
Flower

6　Arranging the Flowers

Making feather flowers carefully is a waste of effort if one fails to display them to their best advantage. Like other artificial flowers, feather flowers have some virtues and some limitations, compared to real flowers. They are not like real flowers and it is a mistake to try to imitate nature too closely when arranging them. Most of the general rules which come naturally to the experienced flower arranger are applicable to feather flowers, but there are certain important differences which ought to be noted.

On the negative side, the feather flower lacks some of the springiness and natural flexibility of a living plant, and the graceful curves which living stems take up have to be *induced* in the artificial arrangement. As a bonus, however, the feather arrangement will have no need of a watertight container, will not drop its petals, will happily stand on a central heating radiator, and will never exhibit the chemical hostility which makes such living flowers as daffodils and tulips antipathetic. Any lack of harmony will be an aesthetic one, and the arranger will be to blame.

Designing with flowers is akin to painting a picture, composing a tune or arranging a dance. The choreographer uses his dancers in groups or singly to form shapes and lines on the stage, and then uses their bodies and arms and legs to create patterns. He can move his dancers about when he wants a change. A composer, too, will orchestrate a theme with variations. Whatever the art form, the artist must know what his tools can do.

A key to success in flower arrangement is the careful choice of flowers and colours. Jumbled profusion, successful in an old-fashioned cottage

garden, has less charm as a flower arrangement, still less if the flowers are artificial. It is necessary to be rigorously selective, and to limit the number of *types* of flower used for an arrangement to three or four. Similarly, the number of colours must be controlled, or the final effect may be a jumbled mass of dots of colour, unsatisfactory however beautiful the individual blooms.

In selecting the types and colours for use, there are certain guidelines which can help. Constrast is of the essence of good floral design. Flower types should be chosen to contrast with their neighbours, and show off the distinctive features of each other. Textures should be contrasting: the smooth with the fluffy, the matt with the shiny, the solid with the transparent. Shape and size should contrast: the round and fat with the tall and thin, the large with the small, the straight with the curved. A frail and delicate harebell will look all the better for being contrasted with a strident sun lily, and the colours of the latter will be enhanced if they are allowed to dominate.

In selecting colour, however, one should look for harmony rather than out-and-out contrast. Complementary (ie opposite) colours can be disturbing in a flower arrangement.

Because it need not contain water, the container or vase for your arrangement can be of almost any size or material. It will nevertheless exert, by its shape, a significant effect on the arrangement. Flat containers are naturally used for table centres, where the arrangement must be low and below eye level. Pedestal containers allow the flower heads to hang down below the level of their stems, and the design to approach a more spherical shape. A traditional vase, though not needed for its

Flowers in a copper jug. *Oasis* was wired—not without a little difficulty—inside this old copper jug. The colour of the copper suggested an apricot colour for the dyed goose cocquille feathers. Two sprays of hops (p 33) blend in tone with the jug, as do the fuchsias (p 87), which have also been made with apricot-coloured feathers. The steel-coloured beads in the heart of the fuchsias match the pale grey pheasant back feathers in the centre. Natural-shaped leaves, three green and white bi-coloured leaf sprays (p 89) and layered leaves (p 95) in two tones of green enlarge the curve of the hops. A simple daisy (p 30) in the centre is made with goose nagoire feathers, partly sprayed with copper.

Crested lanterns

water-carrying abilities, is a good starting-point. It must be heavy enough not to overbalance when the arrangement is made. Remember that the water in a vase of real flowers acts as ballast, and keeps the arrangement from overbalancing.

Having chosen your container, select your flowers with a view to the over-all pattern which they will make. A good composition will have a centre of a single flower or a cluster of blooms, with one or more 'lines' radiating from it. Choose your theme and stick to it. An odd number of flowers, five, seven, or nine, is normally more satisfactory than an even number, though of course they do not have to be arranged symmetrically. A beginner might do well to make three or five blooms, such as poppies, which are to be the major flowers of the arrangement, and to place them first, creating a centre with one bloom or more, and allowing the stems of the others to form the direction lines of the composition. No two blooms should be exactly alike, and it is a mistake for the feather-flower maker to attempt uniformity. Secondary flowers, less dominant in appearance, such as goose lilies, can then be introduced to fill out the shape, and perhaps to emphasise the direction lines of the composition. Then will come the introduction of large special feathers in their natural state. If the composition looks a little too 'tight', a few 'leaves' on long stems, such as willow leaves, will help to soften the design and perhaps extend the outline.

Pearly flowers. Two pearly flowers (p 71) and four buds (p 70) are the only flowers in this arrangement. The ostrich feather and the feather grasses (p 90) help to soften the flowers, and there is also a bow of florists' ribbon.

Aim for an effect of depth (as is seen in a well-planned herbaceous border) by arranging the blooms of the same kind together in layers or planes. If the stem length is varied, this will also help to give a quality of depth. Do not set the flowers too closely together when overlapping them in the composition, but keep them well clear of each other, so that each bloom can be seen as a whole. Remember that an arrangement to be set on a table or shelf against a wall can be composed as a picture, as it will always be seen from one side. If the display is to be free-standing, in the centre of the room, it must look well from all sides, and the quality of depth is even more vital.

The flowers at the edges of the composition will help to define the total shape. No flower arrangement will have a hard-and-fast boundary. Light passes through real petals, making them seem more fragile at the edge of an arrangement than in the centre, and light has the same effect with some of the more delicate feathers. Do not be afraid of turning some of the flowers away from the viewer, or in profile. The impossibility of seeing every detail at a glance is one of the fascinations of a good design.

Feathers and the flowers we make from them need a special kind of display. Because they are slightly translucent, they look quite different when placed on a windowsill from their appearance as a table centre, or lit from in front. Remember, too, that they can come to life when placed in a slight draught, especially the fluffy ones such as ostrich feathers and turkey marabouts.

Though all artificial flowers last indefinitely, most paper ones soon look dusty and become discoloured; not so feather flowers, for they can be cleaned. They are surprisingly resilient, and a soft sable paintbrush can be used to remove persistent dust. If the flowers become damaged, each one can be revived over steam, provided the vein is intact, and the individual feathers can be washed.

No one wants to keep the same arrangement around for ever, but feather flowers can be 'unpicked' and precious feathers saved for re-use.

Design in a box. Tail feathers from a golden pheasant command the centre of attention in this box. Three giant daisies (p 51) are placed horizontally, with a line of six simple daisies (p 30) running between them. Three seed heads (p 103) help to lead the eye up to the top of the composition.

Sunflower in a square. The sunflower design is made inside a circle drawn on a square mount. The feathers are applied layer after layer in circles. Turkey cocquilles provide the outline with cockerel tail feathers between them. Chicken body feathers are placed inside a circle, followed by pheasant red hearts, then goose neck feathers dyed green. In the middle some paler red hearts, with cockerel tail feathers in the very centre. Additionally, curled peacock tail feather barbs are pushed into the inner circle of pheasant red hearts.

Design round a candlestick. The flowers stand in a block of *Oasis* which has been wired to the top of the brass candlestick. Three traveller's joy stems (p 92) entwine the candlestick. In the centre two spider flowers (p 37), two goose lilies (p 32) and an iris (p 59) cluster around a sunburst (p 74). All the feathers have been chosen for their contrasting textures.

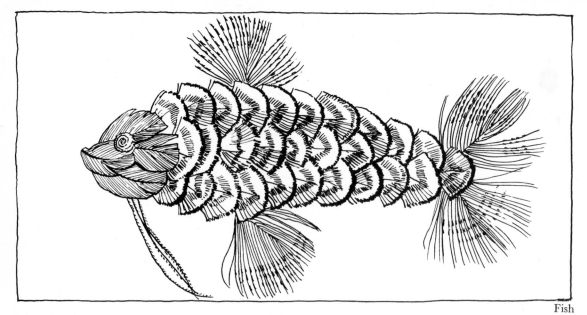

7 *The Fringe of Feathers*

The Victorians, with patience and zeal, would reconstruct the plumage of a bird by gluing feathers as they grew in nature onto an outline of a bird in a picture. This laborious kind of decoration has never had much appeal to me, but designing with feathers need not stop with floral decorations, and feathers are valid materials for wall panels in low relief and two-dimensional designs—feather pictures.

Although a feather is relatively strong and permanent, it is also extremely finely wrought in its detail, and a wall panel using feathers is an admirable way of drawing attention to this.

Feather flowers on a wall panel take up much less space than arrangements, and can easily be stored. Instead of a container, one requires a frame and a baseboard made of stiff cardboard. If feathers are not to be used for the background, a covering of felt or flocked paper of an appropriate colour can be stretched over the cardboard before the flowers are attached.

The flower petals can be glued flat onto the surface of the board. But for a more interesting three-dimensional effect only the centre need be glued, with the petals attached to it in the normal way, so

Wavy stem picture. A wavy line was first drawn on the baseboard as a guide. Overlapping guineafowl feathers were glued along the line, with pheasant tail feathers on one side and double bar partridge feathers on the other. White pigeon body feathers help to emphasise the line. Black cockerel tail feathers cut into tips and laid diagonally form the background.

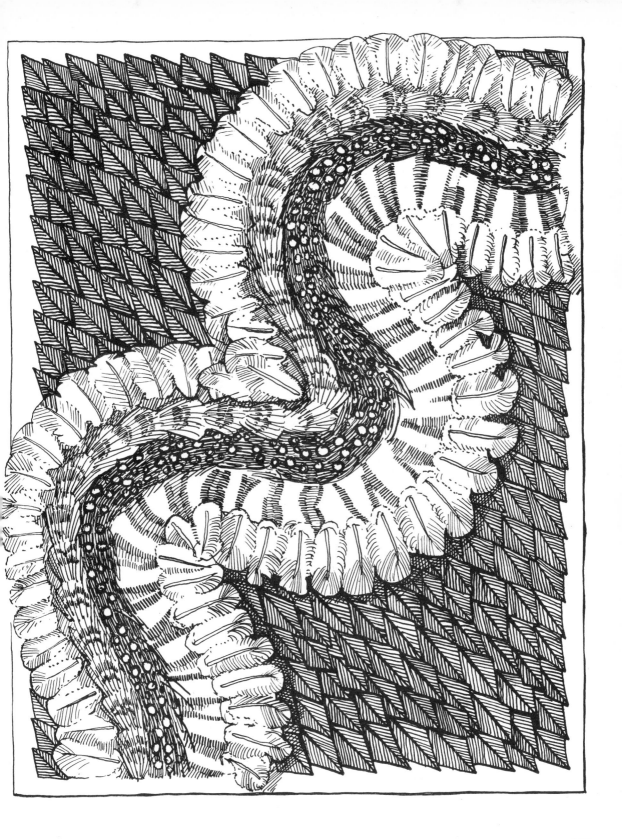

121

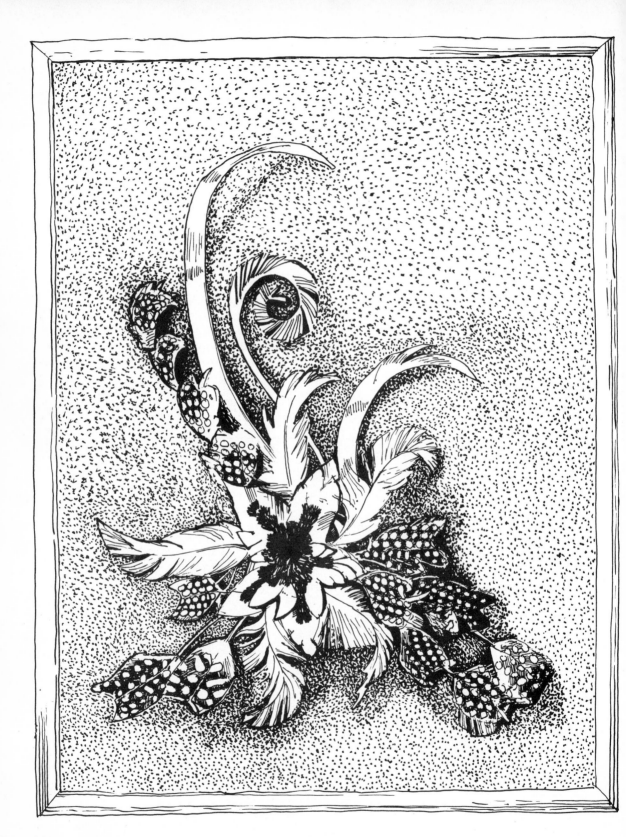

that they stand away from the baseboard. This also allows greater freedom for rearranging the barbs as more flowers are added later.

The technique of making flower panels is very simple, once one has learned to make the flowers themselves. The same rules about contrast in texture, shape and colour apply as in the case of arrangements (chapter 6), although the wall panel is only seen from in front, and is consequently more static and needs to be more formal.

Flowers should be made specially for wall panels; grouping ready-made flowers on a baseboard is not satisfactory. It is not necessary always to make the entire flower. Where flowers overlap, the hidden parts of the bloom should be left out; whole flowers are often too bulky when attached to panels. If all the flowers face the front, the design can become monotonous, and side views of certain flowers are useful in avoiding this. Again it is only necessary to make half a flower that is to be shown in profile, and members of the lily family are the most successful here.

Using the principle by which flowers reflected in a mirror double their apparent size, it is interesting to replace the neutral base material with reflecting acetate foil (see p 125). When using this material, half-flowers seen in profile are seen as whole blooms, and the backs of any free-standing flowers are reflected, adding to the picture's depth. Also reflected, of course, are any flaws and untidy details of construction, and so the workmanship must be good.

Feather wall panels need not contain flowers, and simple abstract patterns can be most striking if made of layers of feathers. The pictures on pp 84 & 124 show some of the patterns which have been created by arranging layers of feathers over geometrical outlines drawn on the base card with compasses. The radial symmetry of the sunflower was of course the starting-point for the picture on p 119. By arranging and gluing feathers in a circle, and overlaying feathers of ever-decreasing size towards the centre, a handsome rosette can be made. The cusped shape of most feathers seems to lend itself to designs based on compass curves, and these can be quite intricate. The undulating diagonal wave in the picture on p 121 was made with compasses.

Small patterned feathers are the most satisfactory for this sort of picture design, and successive layers can effectively be contrasted with

Black and white picture. The background material is black flocked paper which looks like velvet. The main flower in the centre has petals made from duck neck feathers in two colours. The paper mounts are wired, so that the whole shape can undulate, allowing the cockerel hackles to spring out from behind. At the top, the two pheasant tail feathers are stripped on one side and curved over a scissor blade and placed on the design with the wheel tendril between them. All the thirteen curled leaves are guineafowl feathers mounted onto foil acetate and then applied to the picture by gluing the top of the feather side of the leaf to the picture and when dry curling the leaf over and attaching the stem. It is necessary to hold the leaves with pins until the glue is dry.

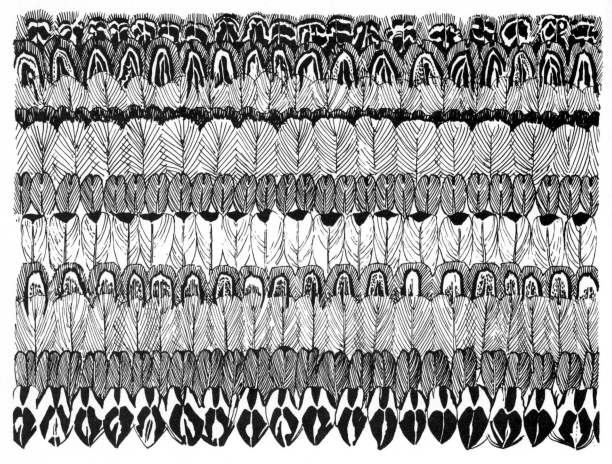

Feather fields. A simple but effective picture made from carefully chosen rows of feathers. The feathers here are all from a ring-necked pheasant and show the surprising variety of its feathers.

Flowers reflected. An interesting effect is produced by the use of foil acetate for the background of this picture. The special feather in the centre comes from the edge of the peacock's tail, where it forms a fringe to the fan of eye feathers. Simple flowers with duck feather petals pushed into the *Oasis* cluster around the base of the feather. Silver beads have been chosen for their centres to match the background. Lines of lily shapes have been made by stripping the brown side of the drake's wing feathers and curving them over a scissor blade. These are arranged in pairs, one feather curving each way and placed on top of the curly drake's tail feather and then all bound together with wire. This binding is hidden by overlapping the feathers slightly. At the top of the picture are three half-flowers each with a centre made of a stripped and cut turkey feather, with three fluffy pigeon feathers below it. Jungle cock body feathers have been used for the petals which are only on one side—the other side appears in the reflection—and the same effect is produced by the two half-flowers made of peacock body feathers and grey pearl duck feathers on the right side of the picture. The balance is altered by the three exotic leaves mounted with peacock body feathers. Finally, two fluffy ostrich body feathers have been added to soften the lines.

an occasional line of plain feathers. If all the feathers in a panel design are chosen from the same bird, such as a pheasant, there is a striking harmony in the result; the design on p 124 was made in this way, and was based on a natural landscape of fields and hedges in level country.

This design covers the whole of the baseboard, but where an abstract pattern leaves an open background a regular arrangement of plain feathers over this area is often better than felt or flocked paper. Like woven cloth, such a feather ground will have a 'grain' according to the direction in which the feathers point, and at right angles to it there will be another direction line made by the lines of feather tips. If the feathers for the background are arranged in diamond pattern, they can be varied, but, generally speaking, a neutral, unobtrusive background is to be preferred.

Layers of overlapping feathers can of course be adapted for other purposes—the design below is made by cutting such a feather ground up into petal shapes. Most interesting, if glued onto cloth or leather, they are flexible and can be used as chokers, belts, even watchstraps, and can be dyed to match or contrast with clothes.

Tiny feathers too small for flowers are handily used up in this way, and anyone who has made the designs in chapters 4 and 5 will have experienced the urge to make use of the colourful scraps which are otherwise cast away.

Flower pattern. This pattern was made by covering an area of paper with six rows of contrasting types of ring-necked pheasant feathers. Then six petal shapes were cut from the rows, and the feathers made good where damaged at the edges. The petals were placed on the picture to form a flower pattern and the centre filled with little coils of ostrich feather barbs. White pigeon feathers applied in rows form the contrasting background.

List of materials other than feathers

		Sources
acetate film	fine transparent plastic sheeting, available in many colours	stationers, Paperchase, H. G. Kettle
binding wire	thin wire or fuse wire, sold on reels	florists, hardware shops, electrical stores
cartridge paper	drawing paper sold in pads	stationers, artists' materials shops
cherries (artificial)		florists
drop beads	glass pendant beads	bead shops, eg Ells & Farrier
dyes	fabric hot water dyes	hardware shops, haberdashers
foil acetate	reflective plastic sheeting	stationers, Paperchase, H. G. Kettle
glue, eg UHU	impact plastic glue	stationers, hardware shops
gutta percha	self-adhesive tape	florists
holly berries (artificial)		florists
Oasis	green plastic foam used in arranging flowers of all sorts	florists
Oasis balls	spheres, ready cut, of *Oasis*	florists
pearl beads		bead shops
puff balls	compressed cotton wool balls, available in many sizes	bead shops
spray paints	supplied in aerosol cans	hardware shops
stem wires	stiff florists' wire, available in 9in, 12in, 18in lengths, light, medium or heavy weights	florists
Styrofoam balls	balls of plastic foam, green or white, various sizes	florists
wire cutters		hardware shops

The addresses of the shops mentioned in the above list are:

Paperchase, 216 Tottenham Court Road, London W1
H. G. Kettle, 127 High Holborn, London WC2
Ells & Farrier, 2 Princes Street, London NW1

Flower Making Index
Arrow Flower, 85
Bead Daisy, 69
Begonia, 77
Cactus Flower, 78
Carnation, 86
Cherry Flower, 43
Clematis, 67
Crested Lantern, 60
Crested Pigeon Lily, 56
Curly Wig Flower, 31
Dewdrop Flower, 62
French Partridge Flower, 73
Frosted Pine Lily, 75
Fuchsia, 87
Giant Daisy, 51
Globe Flower, 40
Goose Lily, 32
Harebell, 48
Hollyhock, 41
Ice Flower, 49
Iris, 59
Jacobean Waterlily, 66
Jonquil, 52
Mallow, 54
Monbretia, 58
Morning Glory, 64
Parrot Tulip, 61
Peacock Flower, 81
Pearly Flower, 71
Pearly Flower Bud, 70
Peony, 63
Periwinkle, 34
Poppy, 55
Protea, 80
Rose, 36
Silver Primrose, 76
Simple Daisy, 30
Snowball, 50
Snowdrop, 44
Spider Flower, 37
Spray of Hops, 33
Star Flower, 47
Stem of Stars, 68
Sunburst, 74
Sun Lily, 83
Tropical Lily, 82
Tulip Marabout, 42
Umbrella Flower, 45

Leaf Making Index
Bicoloured leaves, 89
Biot Palm, 106
Bracken, 110
Bulrush, 97
Couch Grass, 94
Curly Leaves, 104
Disc Leaf, 107
Feather Grass, 90
Helter Skelter Tendril, 96
Layered Leaf, 95
Loop Leaf, 102
Maidenhair Fern, 99
Mimosa Leaf, 109
Seed Head, 103
Simple leaf, 88
Traveller's Joy, 92
Variegated Ivy Leaf, 101
Wheel Tendril, 100
Willow, 91